MW00534431

Eat This Book!

Strength for Your Journey with the Jewish Jesus

Stuart Dauermann

With a Foreword by Russ Resnik

Heart Ally Books, LLC
Camano Island, Washington

Eat This Book!
Copyright ©2022 Stuart Dauermann
All rights reserved, including the right to reproduce this book or portions thereof in any form whatsoever.

Bible quotations used throughout with permission and noted according to the following:
Bible verses designated (ASV) are from the American Standard Version which is in the public domain and were copied from BibleGateway.com.

Various quotations designated (CJB) taken from the Complete Jewish Bible by David H. Stern. Copyright © 1998. All rights reserved. Used by permission of Messianic Jewish Publishers, 6120 Day Long Lane, Clarksville, MD 21029. www.messianicjewish.net.

Scripture quotations marked (ESV) are from The ESV® Bible (The Holy Bible, English Standard Version®), copyright © 2001 by Crossway, a publishing ministry of Good News Publishers. Used by permission. All rights reserved.

Scripture quotations marked (GNT) are from the Good News Translation in Today's English Version-Second Edition Copyright © 1992 by American Bible Society. Used by Permission.

Verses designated (KJV) are from the King James Version which is in the public domain and were copied from BibleGateway.com.

Scripture texts designated (NABRE) in this work are taken from the New American Bible, revised edition © 2010, 1991, 1986, 1970 Confraternity of Christian Doctrine, Washington, D.C. and are used by permission of the copyright owner. All Rights Reserved. No part of the New American Bible may be reproduced in any form without permission in writing from the copyright owner.

Scripture quotations taken from the (NASB®) New American Standard Bible®, Copyright © 1960, 1971, 1977, 1995, 2020 by The Lockman Foundation. Used by permission. All rights reserved. www.lockman.org

Quotations designated (NET) are from the NET Bible® copyright ©1996, 2019 by Biblical Studies Press, L.L.C. https://netbible.com. All rights reserved.

Scripture quotations marked (NIV) are taken from the Holy Bible, New International Version®, NIV®. Copyright © 1973, 1978, 1984, 2011 by Biblica, Inc.® Used by permission of Zondervan. All rights reserved worldwide. www.zondervan.com The "NIV" and "New International Version" are trademarks registered in the United States Patent and Trademark Office by Biblica, Inc.®

Scripture designated (NKJV) taken from the New King James Version®. Copyright © 1982 by Thomas Nelson. Used by permission. All rights reserved.

Scripture quotations marked (NLT) are taken from the Holy Bible, New Living Translation, copyright ©1996, 2004, 2015 by Tyndale House Foundation. Used by permission of Tyndale House Publishers, Carol Stream, Illinois 60188. All rights reserved.

Scripture quotations designated (NRSV) are from New Revised Standard Version Bible, copyright © 1989 National Council of the Churches of Christ in the United States of America. Used by permission. All rights reserved worldwide.

Scripture quotations designated (RSV) are from Revised Standard Version of the Bible, copyright © 1946, 1952, and 1971 National Council of the Churches of Christ in the United States of America. Used by permission. All rights reserved worldwide.

Scripture designated (TLV) taken from the Holy Scriptures, Tree of Life Version*. Copyright © 2014, 2016 by the Tree of Life Bible Society. Used by permission of the Tree of Life Bible Society.

Cover and graphic design by Em Hurley.

Published by:
Heart Ally Books LLC
26910 92nd Ave NW C5-406, Stanwood, WA 98292
Published on Camano Island, WA, USA
www.heartallybooks.com

ISBN-13: 978-1-63107-043-3 (epub)
ISBN-13: 978-1-63107-044-0 (paperback)

2 3 4 5 6 7 8 9 10 11

With thanks to Andrea,
who invited me to the table.

CONTENTS

Foreword vii

Preface xiii

Introduction xv

A Note to the Reader xxi

Chapter One: The Goblet of Prayer 1

Chapter Two: Making a *Motzi*:
  The Bread of the Word 47

Chapter Three: Tasteful Talk 77

Chapter Four: Inviting Others to the Feast 99

Chapter Five: Yeshua's Good News:
  A Well-presented Meal 119

Chapter Six: Room at the Table:
  God's Surprising Guest List 143

Chapter Seven: Light the Lamps!
  The Spirit of the Feast 161

Chapter Eight: *Kashrut*: Mealtime Mindfulness,
  Jewish-Style 189

Chapter Nine: Shabbat: Our Weekend Oasis 215

Chapter Ten: Let's Have a *Meating* 239

Chapter Eleven: Calendar in the Kitchen:
  A Family Affair 263

Chapter Twelve: Cookies on the Top Shelf:
  More on the Hendricks Method 293

Afterword: Would You Like a Glass of Hot Tea? ... 315

Acknowledgments 319

Appendix 321

Bible Abbreviations 321

Sample Horner Bookmarks 324

Notes 327

For Further Reading 339

Also by Dr. Stuart Dauermann 349

FOREWORD

Recently, I spent a few days at a retreat center by a lovely, tree-lined lake in East Texas. I was visiting rabbi with a group of young adults, and our discussions focused on commitment. One morning I spoke about the widespread fear of commitment, and how we can overcome that fear by getting in touch with God's commitment to us. I thought that was a pretty neat phrase and a good way to wrap up my presentation and lead into questions and discussion. The first question that came up was, "You said we can overcome our fear of commitment by getting in touch with God's commitment to us. How do we do that?" I loved that question! It meant my young friends were engaging with me on this topic and ready to explore it more deeply.

The question also reminded me that without the how-to, any message, however neat its punchline, is only pious talk. It might sound good, but is it more than just a sanctified sound bite? Does it point to something real and accessible to actual human beings, and if so, does it provide some concrete guidance on how we get our hands on it?

This practical, how-to element is often missing in spiritual messaging today. We hear aspirational words, but not so much about how to translate these words into changes in the way we live. Like the young questioner at the retreat, lots of younger adults are impatient with religious slogans and taglines and want credible specifics. And older folks often share this perspective as well. If we can't translate our religious admonitions into concrete and specific action items, they might not be ready for broadcast time.

This is where my friend and colleague Rabbi Stuart Dauermann steps up to meet the need. In *Eat This Book!*, Rabbi Stuart marshals a lifetime of learning, practice, and interaction with real-life humans to respond to the how-to questions that arise in areas of spiritual development like Bible study and prayer, sharing the message of Messiah, and practicing redemptive speech.

You might say that Rabbi Stuart answers the most fundamental how-to questions that arise concerning Jewish life with Messiah Yeshua. Messiah taught us "the two most pivotal commandments," as Rabbi Stuart puts it, namely, "loving God with all our hearts, souls, and minds, and also loving our neighbors as we love ourselves." Who can argue with that? But an honest hearer might well ask, as did my young adult friend, "Okay, love God and love my neighbor—but how do I do that?" The same question applies to the Master's equally pivotal and even more concise command: "Follow me."

I'm citing these foundational commandments to point out that *Eat This Book!* isn't only about spiritual practices that we might pursue in a quiet time and place each day (although that's essential), but about the whole journey with the Jewish Jesus, as the subtitle puts it. It's what might be called in other contexts a discipleship manual, something we urgently need in the Messianic Jewish community today. A journey with the Jewish Jesus is going to embrace and affect all of life, and the range of topics in *Eat This Book!* reflects that reality: prayer and scripture study, of course, but also how to avoid malicious or abusive speech, how to talk with others about spiritual things without driving them away, how to keep kosher and Shabbat, and how to be part of *tikkun olam*, "repairing and healing our broken world and the people who share it with us."

As I said, the how-to sort of question makes me, as a teacher, happy, because it means someone is really listening, and because it provides a springboard for deeper discussion. It's also a good Jewish question, not caught up in the theoretical (although there are plenty of good Jewish theoretical questions too), but insisting that we look at the world around us and consider how to live within it more fruitfully.

I just mentioned that *Eat This Book!* might be called a discipleship manual in other contexts. Like how-to questions, the issue of discipleship, or more simply of *following*, reflects a pressing need in our times. If Jesus or Yeshua is going to be relevant at all in this day of materialism, skepticism, and doubt, we can't consider him as a figure merely to be admired or analyzed from afar. We have to engage him on his own terms, which he repeatedly stated simply as, "Follow me." Rabbi Stuart helps us start or keep following, as Yeshua himself so often did, by inviting us to a feast...in this case a feast of teaching and discussion prompts that energize us for the journey ahead. He says his book constitutes "appetizers for people exploring Jewish life Yeshua-style, or Yeshua-faith Jewish style. Above all, we want to make you hungry for more." The array of topics in *Eat This Book!* promise to influence and motivate hungry Jewish followers of Messiah.

I like all these food metaphors, but I'm not so sure about the "appetizer" description. A few years back I was on a teaching assignment in the city of Belo Horizonte, Brazil. I'd study all morning and then teach an intensive course on the Torah from a Messianic Jewish perspective in the evening. And in between, lunch as only Brazil can offer up: *Churrascaria*! This Brazilian barbecue feast is to an ordinary lunch as a firehose is to a squirt gun. You start out at the salad bar, the size of an aircraft carrier, with piles of fresh garden vegetables and more exotic offerings like roasted pineapple, sliced mangoes, and quail eggs. When you sit down, waiters are circulating with skewers of barbecued meat, urging you to try another slice of this steak or that roast, and looking disappointed if you decline. The abundance of Rabbi Stuart's offering makes it the *churrascaria* of books on spiritual formation. As with a Brazilian barbecue house, there's so much there that you'll have to pace yourself, choose what you can handle for now, and keep coming back for more. You'll be glad that return visits are welcome. And so, dear reader, grab your seat at the table and prepare to dig in!

Russ Resnik
Rabbinic Counsel
Union of Messianic Jewish Congregations

PREFACE

They call it an "elevator pitch." It's a brief presentation you might give to someone in an elevator who asks you what you do or what you have in your hand, and whom you answer during your brief ride together. The trick is, keep it short.

So here's my elevator pitch about this book: *"Eat This Book! is a discipling manual that is user-friendly and Judaism-positive."*

A good elevator pitch will arouse more interest, and lead to questions like, "What's a discipling manual? User-friendly for whom? And what do you mean by Judaism-positive?" The answers to these questions are, "A discipling manual is a guide to assist those who want to improve and live out their connection with Yeshua of Nazareth and the God of Israel. This one is user-friendly especially for people with limited knowledge of Jewish life or of the Bible, and even those who know more. And this user-friendly discipling manual is Judaism-positive in that it seeks to help everyone grow in their connection to Jewish life, and in respect for Jewish tradition."

There are lots of good books written by people in our circles such as David H. Stern, David Rudolph, Dan Juster, John Fischer, Jacob M. Rosenberg, Barney Kasdan, Mark Kinzer, Russ Resnik, Jen Rosner, the folks from First Fruits of Zion, Jonathan Bernis, and the scholars connected with mission societies, too, like Mitch Glaser. I admire them all, as I apologize to those I unwittingly left out. I also want to thank people from whom I stole ideas, like Nathan Joiner, who sees liturgy like trail climbing. So do I, and I modified his great idea. All of these efforts are good. But because I still felt there was a need for a discipling manual that was user-friendly and Judaism-positive all at the same time, I wrote one.

Here is a warning! *Eat This Book!* will not get the job done if you just hand it to someone. Discipling is not indoctrination; it is sharing life with God with other people. This book is a foundational tool to help you help others, those near to Yeshua faith, or newly in it, and even those who have been around a while but want to iron out some wrinkles. It should be discussed one on one, or in small groups. And you should take the lead!

Millennia ago, God charged the Prophet Habakkuk to "Write down the vision, make it plain, so that the reader may run with it" (Habakkuk 2:2, TLV). That's what I tried to do.

Now, go and run with it!

Stuart Dauermann
Shavuot 5782

INTRODUCTION

"Our enemies tried to kill us. We survived. Let's eat!" Truth! For Jews, food and faith go together. The Bible hits this note early. Remember the story of Adam, Eve, a tree, and its fruit? Scripture constantly compares life with God to a meal.

The twenty-third Psalm begins with familiar opening words, "The LORD is my shepherd; I shall not want." But the Psalm also exhibits the Bible's faith-food-fixation a few verses later:

> You prepare a table before me
> in the presence of my enemies;
> you anoint my head with oil;
> my cup overflows.
> (Ps 23:5, NIV)

Even most atheists and agnostics would consider a comfortable life with God, complete with a prepared table and an overflowing cup. As an eighteen-year-old agnostic cynic (and still a cynic, but no longer eighteen), I accepted an invitation to this meal of meaning and meeting. And in this book, I want to share the invitation and the meal with you.

The Bible amazes us with the beauty and variety of its invitations to the Feast. The Prophet Isaiah, in the eighth century BCE, is big on inviting people to share in the goodies:

> Come, everyone who thirsts,
>   come to the waters;
> and he who has no money,
>   come, buy and eat!
> Come, buy wine and milk
>   without money and without price.
> (Isa 55:1, ESV)

He envisions the Feast on Mount Zion. The description is mouth-watering, or should I say, "soul-watering"?

> On this mountain the LORD of hosts will
>   make for all peoples a feast of rich food,
>   a feast of well-aged wine, of rich food
>   full of marrow, of aged wine well refined.
> And he will swallow up on this mountain
>   the covering that is cast over all peoples,
>   the veil that is spread over all nations.
>   He will swallow up death forever;
> and the LORD GOD will wipe away tears
>   from all faces, and the reproach of his
>   people he will take away from all the
>   earth, for the LORD has spoken.

> It will be said on that day, "Behold, this is
> our God; we have waited for him, that
> he might save us. This is the LORD; we
> have waited for him; let us be glad and
> rejoice in his salvation."
> (Isa 25:6–9, ESV)

Can you think of a more sumptuous spiritual feast? Who would decline such an invitation?

Isaiah doesn't have a corner on this market. The people in the Newer Testament constantly eat together and talk about food. (Please see an explanation for the term "Newer Testament" in "A Note to the Reader.")

And often they see their meals as a preview of what Isaiah talked about, the End-Time God-Feast. This is why we often see Yeshua (Jesus of Nazareth) eating with people of all kinds, including outcasts and those considered "low-lifes." He is giving us a picture and a preview of the Age to Come and how people of all kinds, even "rejects," will get to sit and schmooze with God's superstars at the End-Time God-Feast!

> Moreover, I tell you that many will come
> from the east and from the west to take
> their places at the feast in the Kingdom
> of Heaven with Avraham, Yitz'chak and
> Ya'akov.
> (Matt 8:11, CJB)

You are right to ask, "What does this have to do with me *now?*" Good question! The good news is that God has a number of ways of feeding us *now* while we wait for the God-Feast. He wants to make sure we don't spiritually starve, although for sure, some people do. In another Psalm, the Bible helps us understand God's desire to feed us, not just later but right now:

> I am ADONAI your God, who brought you
> up from the land of Egypt. Open your
> mouth, and I will fill it.
> (Ps 81:11[10], CJB)

Later in this Psalm he adds that he would feed you with the "finest of the wheat, and with honey from the rock I would satisfy you" (Ps 81:16, ESV).

The book you are reading is something of a spiritual cookbook, providing ways to satisfy your spiritual hunger while waiting for God's Great Feast. If you are just curious, or if you are spiritually famished or just plain hungry, *Eat This Book!* And the way to eat it is to read it, discuss it, understand it, and most of all, put it into practice.

Each chapter presents one or more "dishes" for you to consume. In most cases, these dishes are spiritual practices. And at the end of each chapter, there is a section called "For Better Digestion" consisting of a few questions to help you better digest the chapter. This is followed by a list of resources called "More Food for

Thought," just in case you want to go deeper into the subject at hand. And finally, each chapter ends with a key thought from the chapter, which we call "Take-Out."

To help you ease into each chapter and get a taste of what's ahead for you, each chapter begins with a *nosh*, a taste of what's in store for you. For example, the first chapter is called "A Goblet of Prayer." So your *nosh* will be a taste of the wine of prayer. We could compare this way of beginning each chapter to what is known as *kiddush* (the blessing over the wine to begin Shabbat).

We've done our best to keep the fare light, not telling you everything you ever wanted to know about each dish. *Eat This Book!* is not the last word on the subjects it treats. Compared to God's End-Time Feast, at best these are appetizers for people exploring Jewish life Yeshua-style, or Yeshua-faith Jewish style. Above all, we want to make you hungry for more.

So come! *Ess mein kind! Mangia! B'tei'avon!* Whatever your language, *Eat This Book!* Because you shouldn't starve on the way to the Age to Come!

A NOTE TO THE READER

You will notice the terms "Older Testament" and "Newer Testament" used throughout this book. These terms are employed instead of the conventional "Old" and "New Testament" because the latter terms carry suspicious theological baggage. They are often used to indicate that the New Testament is superior to the Old Testament, which is viewed as being passé. This assumption is linked to "replacement theology" or "supersessionism," which views the Jewish people as having been displaced as the people of God, now replaced by the church from among the nations, a dubious assumption.

Therefore, in this text we use terms indicating chronology and not some pecking order between the Testaments. Some people would refer to the Older Testament as "the Tanakh," and that is a splendid Jewish name for it. Such parties might then refer to the Newer Testament as "The Apostolic Witness," also a splendid term. However, because many reading this book will be new to reading Scripture, I have chosen terms that have a ring of familiarity while avoiding the pecking order of the terms *Old Testament* and *New Testament*. So, instead, we will refer to the Older Testament and Newer Testament.

To keep this book palatable for readers from all different backgrounds and preferences, I have chosen to minimize the number of endnotes and in-text citations to keep the dishes on the table presented as clearly and simply as possible.

Abbreviations used throughout this book for the books of the Bible, as well as for the various versions of the Bible quoted, are identified in the Appendix at the back of this book. For readability, I chose to list the original Hebrew names of each book of the Bible in the Appendix rather than include them along with their English counterparts in every Scripture citation in the book. I encourage you to familiarize yourself with these original Hebrew names for the books of the Bible.

Following the Appendix, you will find the full reference information for each book or resource cited in the text arranged alphabetically by author in the For Further Reading section.

You will notice that I frequently quote Scripture verses from the *Complete Jewish Bible* (CJB), and occasionally, that version will have alternate numbering of some verses from the conventional numbering system in most Christian Bible versions. When you see something like 14[10], it shows the original number of the verse in the Hebrew text first, followed by the standard numbering used in most Christian translations in brackets.

CHAPTER ONE

THE GOBLET OF PRAYER

Prayer Walking: A *Nosh* of Prayer

Prayer walking is a way of enfolding prayer into your day in an effective and unobtrusive manner as if talking to someone on the phone. I promise you will find it to be a welcome and useful habit. Especially in an area like New York City where everyone walks miles every week, it is an excellent way to use that time as an opportunity to chat with God.

We are all used to seeing people on the street using earphones, ear plugs, or a Bluetooth device to talk on the phone. We don't assume they are crazy and talking to themselves! Most of us have such headphones, earbuds, or Bluetooth devices. But here's a great idea! Why not place them in your ear and talk with *God* as you walk? Who will know that your connection is to his area code?

Nobody will call 911 on you! And it works just as well in the suburbs as it does in Times Square. Whatever is on your heart, talk it out with God. This is prayer walking.

This is also something you can do with someone else. In this variation, as you walk on the busy streets, while you each appear to be talking to each other, you can alternate talking with God. It's really invigorating. Try it today!

Now that we've had a taste, let's talk some more about the goblet of prayer. It is so enriching you won't want to pass it up! We'll start with the why, and proceed to the what of prayer.

The WHY of Prayer

Prayer is spending time with *Avinu Malkenu*, our Father and our King. It creates a space in our lives to contemplate who he is and who we are. It's a way to be guided and empowered for living as his children and his servants. Prayer is not a performance. It is not a religious routine. *Prayer is a way of keeping company with God.*

It has taken me a lifetime to catch all of this. For about fifty years I prayed three kinds of extemporaneous prayers:

• *I'm sorry prayers.* These were prayers of confession asking for forgiveness. These were episodic—from time to time, as the occasion demanded. And they were frequent!

• *Bless this prayers.* These were prayers asking God to enhance some sermon I was about to preach, some lesson I was going to teach, some mentoring of a person who had come to me for help, or some pet project.

• *Summary prayers.* These were the prayers I would pray at the end of a teaching, summarizing what we had learned and sending people off to live it out. They were really summaries for the people attending, under the guise of addressing God.

If you find these ways of praying too transactional and not relational enough, you will get no argument from me. All of this is too self-centered, treating God as our backup man. Sorry! That won't do! If prayer is a way of keeping company with God, spending time with our Father and our King, you will find yourself bumping into the emphatically supernatural. Yes, prayer is the context where this is most likely to happen. Getting thirsty for this wine yet?

Transactional approaches to prayer fail because the God to whom we pray demands and deserves to be central in our lives, the Hub from whom all else proceeds. The Apostle Paul says, "he who is joined to the Lord becomes one spirit with him" (1 Cor 6:17, ESV). Our spirit is our deepest intrinsic self, and when we come into maximized relationship with God through allegiance to Yeshua, his Spirit, God's essential Self, bonds with our own. The beingness of God is bonded with our beingness. All of life is governed by what goes on here.

But prayer is not only an atmosphere and a meeting. It is a kind of activity. How should we then pray?

The WHAT of Prayer

Because prayer is deeply relational, it is also highly personal. Therefore, each of us will tend to favor one or more styles of prayer over the others surveyed here. Let's take a look at some varieties of prayer.

WHAT: Pray the Bible

Prayer and reading the Bible are not meant to be separate and sealed off from each other! No! Reading Scripture and engaging in prayer flow into each other, creating wellsprings of meaning, joy, insight, and power. It's naturally supernatural. Again, as you read, convert your insights into prayer.

Let me help you get a feel for this. Here are six cues that will launch this kind of prayer for you and keep it flying. They all begin with the letter "R."

Reflect. This is the first thing you should do. Reflect on the meaning of that text, using skills we will discuss in our next chapter on Bible reading. The goal here is simply to track with the meaning of the text as best we can.

Repent. If the text points out a sin to avoid, then use the text to express your repentance. Personalize the text. Apply it to yourself. Speak it to God in the first person.

Resolve. Does the text remind you of something you ought to resolve to do? A commandment to obey,

4

a promise to make and keep? If so, do it here, and jot it down so you don't forget.

Rejoice. Is there something here to celebrate, for which to give thanks and praise to God? If so, make the words of Scripture your own and reflect all of this back to God.

Request. Is your reading suggesting something you want to ask of God? Some request for his help or intervention? Personalize the text, using it as basis for asking something of God. He delights to hear the prayers of his children.

Remember. There will be some texts you want to remember, and this is very life-giving. Jot down the text, either copying it, or just noting its reference. This becomes something upon which to meditate and something to memorize. It's a good thing!

Please don't feel like you have to turn these six R's into rules to follow. They are instead helpful prompts to inspire and assist you in your practice of Bible-connected prayer. It's really the most naturally supernatural thing imaginable. Soon you will learn to flow from reading into praying and back again, over and over, because that's the way God designed it to be.

WHAT: *Hitbodedut*

This is a good modality of prayer for introverts.

Perhaps you saw the movie *Ushpizin* about a poor Hasidic Jewish couple, Moshe and Malli, living in Jerusalem. The movie traces their adventures with God and also with unexpected guests during the festival of Sukkot. At one point in the film, Moshe gets stressed out, but wants to avoid reverting to old patterns of rage. So, he runs through the streets and out into the nearby woods to cry out to God. What is this?

This is *hitbodedut*, a prayer modality Rebbe Nachman of Breslov taught centuries ago to his followers. Nachman, who lived around the time of Ludwig van Beethoven in the late 1700s, was a genius about the psychology of spirituality. He intuitively understood the discouragements that hinder spiritually questing people.

Of course, as religious Jews, his followers already prayed every day using the prayers of the *siddur*, the Jewish prayerbook. But Nachman knew something more was needed. Therefore, he advised his *hasidim* to practice *hitbodedut*, "voluntary self-seclusion," a time to go off and pray not in community, but alone. He told them to spend an hour a day, gauged as one-twelfth of their daylight hours, and therefore, not always sixty minutes, in unstructured conversational prayer, pouring out their hearts to God in their own language, as a child to a parent. This is spending time with God, crying out to him as our Father and our King.

Rebbe Nachman added that even if we don't know what to say during that time, just giving that time to pursuing him is more precious to God than the worship of all the angels. He told his disciples that this enterprise was best done out of doors. And where he lived, this meant walking alone in the forest. In that time and place, the forest was the best place to go to be alone with God.

Rebbe Nachman sometimes refers to this practice as *sichah beino le-vein kono*—conversation between oneself and one's Owner (God).[1] But it's also a time for talking with ourselves and about ourselves. It is conversation occurring in the space between ourselves and God. In keeping with the meaning of the term *l'hitpallel*, often translated as "to pray," but really meaning to judge oneself, *hitbodedut* is a time of heightened self-awareness and a time of heightened God-awareness—contemplating our God and ourselves in the Light of his Presence.

Yeshua of Nazareth himself practiced this form of prayer, employing it to clarify his priorities and choices. Before he chose his twelve disciples, he spent a night alone in prayer:

> In these days he went out to the mountain to pray, and all night he continued in prayer to God. And when day came, he called his disciples and chose from them twelve, whom he named apostles.
> (Lk 6:12–13, ESV)

Another text reports how he got up extra early one morning to spend a protracted time in prayer to get clarity on his priorities:

> And when it was day, he departed and went into a desolate place. And the people sought him and came to him, and would have kept him from leaving them, but he said to them, "I must preach the good news of the kingdom of God to the other towns as well; for I was sent for this purpose."
> (Lk 4:42–43, ESV)

This was Yeshua's habitual mode of guidance and empowerment. Who would not want to imitate his example? Here's how:

• Pick a place where you can be alone, undistracted and undisturbed, preferably out of doors. In Rebbe Nachman's day, that place would be in the forest or in the fields. I found my place to be walking the streets of my suburban neighborhood during hours when hardly anyone would be out. (As for the urban environment, another approach is in order, as we saw in the option of walking on the street having a Bluetooth-aided conversation with God.)

• If outdoors is just not workable for you, indoors is fine. But again, you will want to be undisturbed, allowing you to talk out loud.

- Calendar this time: Make it specific. We should schedule our appointments with God the same way we schedule an appointment with anyone else. Otherwise, believe me—busyness will crowd him out. Yeshua was the busiest of people. He did his *hitbodedut* before sunrise, or in the night when no one was around.
- Then, just talk with God. It takes time to sense his responses, but he does respond. I recognize his feedback as an incisive and nonintrusive wisdom that arises within me that is greater than my own and that, when followed, makes headway in my life. It also increases my sense of freedom. As Paul put it, "And where the Spirit of ADONAI *is*, there is freedom" (2 Cor 3:17, CJB).

Here's an example of how this works. I was driving to a meeting where I would be teaching, and I fell into the dysfunctional pattern I mentioned at the start of this chapter: I prayed a "bless this" prayer, asking God to add his blessing to what I had already prepared. Right away I found myself checked. I realized this was wrong; I shouldn't have been praying that God would bless what I was about to do. Instead, I should have been praying, "Lord what do you want to do in this situation and how can I be an instrument of your purpose for these people?" Immediately, I had a sense of how I needed to posture myself on that occasion, and the whole day was more productive as a result. Prayer is not a monologue. It's a dialogue. It takes time, practice, and attention to learn to detect the subtle, yet powerful, ways God interacts with us—that is, if we will make ourselves available.

WHAT: Following Yeshua's Model— The *Avinu* Armature

Most of us will know, at least in part, the familiar "Lord's Prayer," which some call "The Disciples' Prayer" because it was a prayer Yeshua gave to us for our prayer life. This prayer, which is actually a pattern for prayer, is like an armature, the framework a sculptor uses around which clay is formed into a work of art. This is what these words are for us: a framework to be used to shape our prayers. It is amazing how flexible and enduring it is. Here are the words as Matthew records them:

> Our Father in heaven,
> hallowed be your name.
> Your kingdom come.
> Your will be done,
> on earth as it is in heaven.
> Give us this day our daily bread.
> And forgive us our debts,
> as we also have forgiven our debtors.
> And do not bring us to the time of trial,
> but rescue us from the evil one.
> (Matt 6:9–13, NRSV)

These thoughts may be used to structure your prayers on just about any matter of concern you might have. They serve as lampposts illumining the situation about which you are praying. The *Amidah*, the core prayer section of Jewish liturgical prayer, is another amazing armature. But more of that later.

As an example of how to use a prayer framework, let's say you are praying for a neighbor friend who has just tested positive for some disease. Here is an outline of how you might pray for her, using the Lord's Prayer, the *Avinu* Armature, as your framework. Let's call your neighbor Adrian, and her husband is Robert.

"Our Father in heaven." You would begin by reminding yourself who it is you are addressing, and what kind of a Father he is. "Father, I pray for Adrian, remembering that you are a compassionate father who loves her very much...." Of course, you would use your own words here, and throughout.

"Hallowed be your name." Here you might pray that God's Name, his reputation, would be advanced in this situation. You would ask him to act in mercy and power for the sake of his reputation, bringing healing to Adrian and comfort to Robert and the children, Nathan, Claire, and Ben.

"Your kingdom come, your will be done on earth as it is in heaven." This is where you remember to pray that God's kingdom, his rulership, and his reign would be manifest in healing Adrian's sickness, here on earth, in the same way that his will is immediately accomplished in heaven.

"Give us this day our daily bread." You could pray that God would supply whatever Adrian and her family need today to keep them in life and health, including sound medical advice and comfort for the children, Robert, and their friends.

"And forgive us our debts as we also have forgiven our debtors." Here you might pray that God would deal with her as a forgiving God, just as she has always been quick to forgive others. You would ask God to forgive and overlook whatever shortcomings she might have.

"And do not bring us to the time of trial." This is where you ask that God would keep Adrian and her loved ones from encountering more than they can handle in this situation.

"But rescue us from the evil one." Here the prayers focus on Adrian's protection from wicked forces that would love to capitalize on her greater vulnerability and stress, and that of her family. Pray for a shield of protection around them at this time.

Or course this is just an example of how these portions of the Lord's Prayer, these lampposts, would illumine just about any situation you might care to pray about. Be as flexible as you want with these lampposts, just making sure that your words reflect the themes of each.

You are likely to feel some closure as you touch all these bases with creativity and flexibility for any number of matters you would pray about. Of course, nobody is saying you have to do things this way! Rather, this is a good approach to use when you are not exactly sure how to proceed, but you feel you ought to pray about some matter that has come to your attention. Think of this as a tool, and a very good one. No wonder—it came from the Master Craftsman himself!

WHAT: Liturgical Prayer

In writing to the Ephesians, Paul says, "pray at all times, with all kinds of prayers and requests, in the Spirit, vigilantly and persistently, for all God's people" (Eph 6:18, CJB). He is calling us to be "multi-style pray-ers." While many people dismiss liturgical prayer as monotonous, irrelevant, and deadening, they don't realize that there are many ways to pray, suited to every kind of temperament. Different styles of prayer, like different forms of exercise, develop different aspects of our spirits. For this reason, liturgical prayer should always have a part to play in our spiritual health, even if there are other forms of prayer "exercise" we practice with more enthusiasm.

Jewish liturgical prayer is called *davening*. What is *davening*? The term refers to using the prayers of the traditional *siddur* (prayer book) to structure and fuel one's prayers. A *siddur* is a set order of prayers. These prayers have evolved over the centuries. However, we have reason to believe they are rooted in the practice of priests and Levites in Temple times. Conservative Jewish scholar Reuven Hammer writes:

The earliest reference we have to an order of prayer is found in a section of the Mishnah Tamid 5:1. It is the record not of a public service, but of a private one conducted by the priests alone.

Describing the way in which the daily morning sacrifice, the *tamid*, was offered, the Mishna tells us that after completing the sacrifice, the priests left the sacrificial court and went down to the Hall of Hewn Stone, a chamber in the Temple complex which was used for large gatherings, including the meeting of the Great Court (the Sanhedrin). This room was not part of the sacred area of sacrifice or the public courts in which people stood to witness the ritual.... The leader said to them, 'Recite one blessing' and they blessed. They recited the Ten Declarations, '*Sh'ma*,' 'And it shall come to pass.' 'And He said... 'They blessed the people with three blessings: 'True and steadfast,' 'The service,' and the blessing of the Priests. (All of these are prayer units still used in Jewish liturgical prayer).

> In other words, sometime prior to the year
> 70 CE, [when the Temple was destroyed]
> there already existed an order of prayer, a
> *siddur*, if you will, for a service that was
> recited daily by the priests.[2]

Traditionally, Jews prefer to *daven* in company with other Jews. This happens three times a day, reflecting the times sacrifices were offered in the Temple. Many Jews will, however, do this alone, exercising flexibility according to personal preference.

Davening is not meant to be a lockstep experience. Think of it like using love songs developed by our community for contemplating and communicating with our Beloved.

Let me boost your interest in *davening* by sharing an edited version of what I wrote for the website of the Messianic Jewish Rabbinical Council. See if you identify with any of the points I make here. Here are seven benefits we derive from liturgical prayer. How many of these make sense to you?

First, we need to *daven* because it puts us in "a different space," a communal space where we reconnect with our identity as members of a kingdom of priests and a holy nation. Grounding ourselves in that self-awareness can, should, and likely will condition everything we do in our day-to-day life.

Second, we need to *daven* to obey *HaShem*'s call upon Israel to bring offerings of praise. Surely, we come into the Presence of the Holy One through the sacrifice of Messiah. But that is not the only sacrifice to bear in mind. Hebrews 13:15 (CJB) reminds us "Through him (that is, through Yeshua), ...let us offer God a sacrifice of praise continually." The writer to the Hebrews says that in entering God's presence through Yeshua's sacrifice, we bring other sacrifices with us—the sacrifice of praise, which situates us squarely in Jewish liturgical prayer practice, which is predominantly praise. *Davening* actualizes and connects us with who God created us to be.

Third, we need to *daven* because otherwise we are left to our own devices in seeking to express and nurture our spirituality. Like most others, we will default to individualism. But when we *daven*, we participate in the world of Jewish prayer together with other Jews throughout time, sharing with them the priestly burdens, privileges, and responsibilities of the people of Israel.

Fourth, we need to *daven* because the depth and diversity of the liturgy speaks to us in different ways each time we pray our prayers. Although the liturgy remains the same, the experience is always different because we are different. The liturgy provides a valuable measuring rod by which to take notice of how we are different today from yesterday, and, even different from all of our yesterdays—and also how we, like the liturgy, remain the same through all our changes.

Fifth, we need to *daven* because God says, "Seek my face." Showing up for such prayer is like having a regular audience with the King of all kings, and we will often find ourselves smiling as we go into it. It is not as if we generate that Presence out of our own subjectivity, but rather we find God there, almost as if God waits to meet us at our regular meeting place.

Sixth, we need to *daven* because we need the companionship of the tradition. There is a holy specialness, a different texture and awareness that *davening* brings, a sense of being part of a global transgenerational community. In praying within the tradition, we are never socially alone, even if we are praying by ourselves at home.

Seventh, we need to *daven* because our role is indispensable to the purposes of God. In the *Tanach*, all sacrifices were to be seasoned with salt. Yeshua told his *talmidim*, his disciples, "You are the salt of the earth; but if salt has lost its taste, how shall its saltiness be restored? It is no longer good for anything except to be thrown out and trampled under people's feet" (Matt 5:13, ESV). We are the salt on the sacrifices of the prayers of Israel—that is part of our function in the world. The only question is, will we play our part?[3]

Of course, there is a learning curve in *davening*. But we can only begin from where we are. It is the same for all of us. We should never shame ourselves about our level of progress, nor allow others to goad us. Each of us must find our way home to the liturgy by our own route and at our own pace. The important thing is to find the road and explore it. No matter how far we are along the road, or how slow or fast we are going, there we meet each other, our tradition, and the God of our ancestors who waits for us there.

Liturgical prayer gets bad press. And some people do all they can to discourage us while we may be just getting acquainted with the process. You know these kinds of people—tour guides on a shortcut to misery!

Jewish Prayer Fallacies: Avoid These Traps

Here are seven traps they love to set, and how to avoid them.

1. "You have to say everything, or it doesn't count." When you encounter punctilious people who want to hit you over the head with this advice, just duck and back away. No, you don't have to say everything! And who's counting anyway?

2. "You have to keep up." Not necessarily! Suppose you are praying with others and some passage "grabs you." In that case, just hang out there for a while, let the passage speak to you, chew on it, pray it, let it live in you.[4]

3. "Say all the words even if you don't understand them." This is what Rabbi Abraham Joshua Heschel called "religious behaviorism," which he viewed to be worthless and stultifying. Better to remember this is a prayer journey, and to follow it with the freedom to be

who you are where you are in the process. This is life-giving. Playing a role is a killer. The assimilated German Jewish philosopher Franz Rosenzweig was once asked if he put on *tefillin*. He responded, "Not yet." This indicated that he was on the road of Jewish observance, pointed in a direction, but was satisfied being *who* he was *where* he was. And so it is for you: Allow yourself to be in process, to be who you are, and to be wherever you are on the journey. And don't let anyone ruin the trip with their micromanagement!

4. "There's no room for the Spirit in such a tightly structured format." People who propose this are restricting the Spirit to spontaneity. A fallacy. The Bible disagrees. In 2 Chronicles Chapter 5, the pomp and pageantry when Solomon's Temple was dedicated is described. No event in all of the Bible is more scripted and regimented than this one. If the objection to a tightly structured format was true, we would expect this Temple dedication to have been spiritually Deadsville. Instead, we read this description:

> And when the priests came out of the Holy Place (for all the priests who were present had consecrated themselves, without regard to their divisions, and all the Levitical singers, Asaph, Heman, and Jeduthun, their sons and kinsmen, arrayed in fine linen, with cymbals, harps, and lyres, stood east of the altar with 120 priests

who were trumpeters; and it was the duty
of the trumpeters and singers to make
themselves heard in unison in praise and
thanksgiving to the LORD), and when the
song was raised, with trumpets and cym-
bals and other musical instruments, in
praise to the LORD,

"For he is good,
    for his steadfast love endures forever,"
the house, the house of the LORD, was
filled with a cloud, so that the priests
could not stand to minister because of the
cloud, for the glory of the LORD filled the
house of God.
(2 Ch 5:11–14, ESV)

In the midst of all this pomp and pageantry, God
shows up and all bets are off. The Holy One obviously
does not have a problem with structured, formal prayer
when it's presented as a love-offering from his people.
He loves to show up in such settings, and nobody is
better than he is at being the Life of the party!

At its worst, pomp and pageantry is pretentious.
But at its best, it embodies the holy decorum appropriate to the courts of the King of Kings.

We're talking about the direct opposite of boring!

5. "It's all vain repetition." Wrong again! Not all repetition is vain repetition. When someone tells their be-

loved, "I love you, I love you, I love you," are the second and third "I love you's" vain repetition? I don't think so!

6. "It's unthinkable to use prayers devised by rabbis who didn't believe in Yeshua." This is an objection cobbled together out of misguided notions that the rabbis have nothing to teach us, and that if you scratch a rabbi, underneath you will find a Christ-killer. (No, that wasn't a nice thing to say. But unfortunately, for many people, this is the usual unexpressed opinion.)

It was Yeshua himself who told us, "The Torah-teachers and the *P'rushim*...sit in the seat of Moshe. So whatever they tell you, take care to do it. But don't do what they do, because they talk but don't act!" (Matt 23:2–3, CJB). Yeshua is telling his disciples that the Jewish religious leaders, the proto-rabbis, and later the rabbis following them, have the God-given authority to interpret Torah. We are to take care to do whatever they tell us to do, but not to repeat their bad examples, because, as other translations put it, "they do not practice what they teach." Behind that latter statement is this assumption: What they teach is valid.

Of course, Yeshua is not saying that the rabbis are always right in all of their teachings. Certainly, there will come times when we cannot agree with what they teach, chiefly when their teaching conflicts with that of Yeshua and his *sh'lichim* (emissaries, apostles). But in the main, we are to see their teachings as authoritative as to what it means to live a Jewish life, one that honors our covenantal identity as the people to whom the Torah was given.

7. "The *siddur* is full of kabbalistic Jewish magic. You've got to be extremely careful." Such statements are usually secondhand rumors repeated by those with little or no actual contact with the *siddur* (the Jewish prayerbook) and how it is used. There are actually very few kabbalistic Jewish prayers to be found there, and these are not Jewish magic. They involve creatively envisioning God's throne room, and similar matters. Certainly, there are some kabbalists who use incantations, amulets, and various forms of folk religion. But this is fringe behavior, common in many religious cultures. But to say that the *siddur* is "full of kabbalistic Jewish magic" is a scare tactic that labels proponents as ignorant and biased. Not good.

Taking the Journey of Jewish Liturgical Prayer

A prayerbook is a map we use to retrace our people's communal prayer experience. If at first you have trouble following it, just remember—that's how it is with maps. For everyone. Reading a map takes skill and experience.

But after reading the map, you need to take the trip it describes or you haven't had any encounter at all! You don't experience San Francisco, New York, or Jerusalem by studying maps. You need to visit! And if we would make the journey of Jewish communal prayer

our own, we should prepare for the journey, study the map, and take the trip.

Preparing for the Journey

This step is like going to the gym to get in shape for a hiking vacation. Here's what you need to do: For two or three weeks, three times a week, take just 15–30 minutes to pray in your own words, following these seven steps. These will make you accustomed to the shape of Jewish liturgical prayer. Be sure to keep it simple, and for most of us, keep it brief. Like being a beginner at a gym, you don't want to kill your motivation by trying too hard. Take it easy. Here are the seven steps, and if it is your style, you may want to take these steps in a diary or journal. But if not, then just follow them out loud. It will take far less time.

Step One—Begin by giving thanks for the gift of a new day. Acknowledge your gender and your identity as a Jew in the stream of worldwide Jewish historical experience.

Step Two—Praise God using Scripture, poetry, and song, perhaps with your own words interspersed.

Step Three—Verbalize your allegiance to God and your desire to follow his will in all of life. (Traditionally, Jewish people do this by reciting the *Sh'ma*).

Step Four—Stand in God's presence, praising him, making requests of him, and thanking him.

Step One	Begin by giving thanks for the gift of a new day, acknowledge your gender, your identity as a Jew in the world and in the stream of Jewish historical experience.
Step Two	Praise God using scripture, poetry, song, or your own words.
Step Three	Verbalize your allegiance to God and your desire to follow his rulings in all of life. (Traditionally, Jewish people do this by reciting the *Sh'ma*).
Step Four	Stand in God's presence, offer him praise, thanks, and prayers.
Step Five	Talk to God about your shortcomings, remind yourself of his forgiveness and provision, and accept these gifts from his hand.
Step Six	Read some passage(s) of Scripture as guidance for today's God-honoring living.
Step Seven	Transition into your day by speaking out some insight you gained from this exercise. Say a prayer and go meet your day!

Step Five—Talk to God about your shortcomings, remind yourself of his forgiveness and provision, and accept these gifts from his hand.

Step Six—Read some passage(s) of Scripture as guidance for today's God-honoring choices.

Step Seven—Transition into your day by speaking out some insight you gained from this exercise. Say a prayer, and go meet your day!

Do this exercise at least three days a week for two or three weeks. This exercise is already bringing you into step with Jewish prayer! As an added bonus, it can also be done in company with others. You will find that this series of steps strengthens you for a life of prayer.

In my role as your personal trainer, here are some pointers about how to make these exercises work for you.

1. At this stage in your prayer journey, as at every subsequent stage, respect your own comfort level. Keep things meaningful and understandable. And yes, it's a good idea to stretch your capacities just a little bit—but not too much. Fight the urge to bite off more than you can chew: It's a motivation-killer. Remember, it's important to enjoy the journey.

2. Part of what makes this a journey on holy ground is elevating our awareness, what Buddhism calls "mindfulness." Jewish tradition reminds us to "Know before whom you are standing"—in other words, re-

member that you have come here to meet with God, the King above all kings. Be mindful of the moment.

3. Just as there is proper dress for going on the gym floor, there is proper dress for going into the Presence of God. Dress appropriately out of respect for the nature of the event. This won't mean wearing your best suit, but it should mean being respectfully clothed. So, if possible, reserve prayer for after you have showered/bathed, and dressed for your day. Making a habit of this will make your prayer time more rewarding. Trust me on this.

4. If you know how to wear a tallis/tallit, kippah, and tefillin, use them.

5. Pick an appropriate place—clean, undistracting, and private. Pray toward the east if you can discover where it is. (Hint: Where is the morning sun?)

6. A lighted candle and even incense are splendid mood-setters.

7. Each day, take a minute or two to jot down what you may have learned, sensed, or heard, as well as any lingering thoughts remaining from your time of prayer. And keep it simple. There's always tomorrow.

8. After spending two to three weeks (more if you want to) experimenting at this level, we will move on to the *siddur* itself.

The Journey Itself

About a mile from my home you will find a mountain trail. Although the trail stays the same, the experience of hiking on it is always different. Perhaps you will stop at different places. Perhaps your experience will be different because one day you are elated, but on another you are preoccupied. And hiking the trail varies depending upon who goes with you and who you meet on the way.

It is the same with Jewish prayer. The prayers remain the same, but you are different every day. Different in your feelings. Different in your experience. Different in what you have been learning. Different because of who goes with you. Returning to our earlier metaphor of going to the gym, the machines are the same, the weights are the same, and the exercises are the same. But because you are different each time, you will approach your workout differently and come away differently changed and strengthened.

On the next page, I sketch and describe the mountain trail of Jewish prayer. The mountain peak toward which we climb is Mount Sinai, because the trail takes us up to receive Torah all over again—instruction for life as servants of Israel's God. This sketch, or map, marks off the landmarks on the journey, following the contours you experienced in the preparations outlined earlier, contours which were modeled after the trail itself.

Landmark 1	Birchot HaShachar
Landmark 2	Pesukei d'Zimra
Landmark 3	The *Sh'ma* Section
Landmark 4	Amida
Landmark 5	Tachanun
Landmark 6	The Torah Section
Landmark 7	Concluding Prayers

In keeping with tradition, the morning service of Jewish prayer has seven landmarks. I will describe the trail of prayer as it is followed on Mondays, Thursdays, and Shabbat. It is slightly different on the other days of the week, but by all means you are free to use this model every day if you choose.

First landmark—*Birchot HaShachar* (Blessings of the Morning) giving thanks for the gift of a new day, acknowledging your gender and identity as a Jew in the stream of worldwide Jewish historical experience. These prayers include *Modeh Ani*, where we give thanks for waking up at all, putting on tallit and tefillin; *Ma Tovu*, giving thanks for the privilege of coming into God's presence; and fifteen blessings reflecting our place in God's created world. Take time—days, weeks, months—to familiarize yourself with all of these. Get comfortable with them one by one. Remember, you are bringing yourself along on this trip, so don't feel obliged to do things that leave yourself behind! Go at your pace and make it meaningful.

Second Landmark—*Pesukei d'Zimrah* (Passages of Praise) in which you praise God using Scripture, poetry, and song, perhaps with your own words interspersed. This is a very extensive section, including praises of God, from all over the *Tanach*. We tend to read these quite rapidly in a kind of scan reading that may be compared to a plane going down the runway. In the process, certain themes recur, and from day to day, different themes will stand out for us. As we continue with this rapid prayer-reading, eventually we attain lift-off. We sense a shift in our consciousness, subtle but real.

The *Pesukei d'Zimrah* begins with *Baruch She'amar* (Blessed Is He Who Spoke and the World Came into Being) giving thanks for God's creative and sustaining mercy. It includes a prayer called the *Ashrei* which incorporates all of Psalm 145. It finishes with a prayer, *Yishtabach.* Learn to rummage around in this long section. Say the prayers out loud.

At first, all of this will seem humdrum. As the Talmud says, "all beginnings are hard," but stick with it, going easy on yourself. Eventually you will attain lift-off. And you will smile. I promise.

Third Landmark—The *Sh'ma* Section where you verbalize your allegiance to God and your desire to follow his will in all of life. The section begins with a call to attention, the *Barchu.* This alerts us that we are about to engage in serious business—pledging faithfulness to the true and living God. The *Sh'ma* begins, "Hear O Israel, the LORD our God is One LORD" followed by "Blessed be his glorious Name forever and ever." Then three paragraphs, the first of which, called the *V'ahavta,* begins, "And you shall love the LORD your God with all your heart, with all your soul, and with all your might." These paragraphs are some of the small print describing what we mean by pledging our loyalty to the God of Israel.

Fourth Landmark—The *Amidah* (the Standing Prayer) in which you stand in God's presence, praising him, making requests of him, and thanking him. Our tradition reminds us that we are a Kingdom of Priests, and a priest brings sacrifices. This is where we do it, bringing to him our sacrifice of praise and thanksgiving. Most days, the *Amidah* begins with three blessings of praise, followed by categorized request-blessings, followed by three more blessings of thanksgiving. This entire set of ingenious blessings outlines God's mercies to his people past, present, and future.

The thirteen request-blessings touch upon nearly every area of human life. You can treat this like a prayer agenda you bring into your meeting with God. And if some prayer or blessing especially arrests you, feel free to linger there whether for understanding, appreciation, or due to a special sense of spiritual connection. On Shabbat and on Festivals, this middle section of thirteen request-blessings is replaced by a single blessing that honors the particular holy day, for example, Shabbat. For a well-organized article supplying more information on the *Amidah* and its various modifications, see Wikipedia.

Fifth Landmark—The *Tachanun* (Supplication) where you talk to God about your shortcomings, remind yourself of his forgiveness and provision, and accept these gifts from his hand. This is a time of humbling ourselves, remembering our failures and mistakes, then seeking and finding God's patience and forgiveness. In a time when so much religious talk is triumphalist, this prayer is so healthy, grounding us in the realities of our neediness and the majesty of how God mercifully forgives us despite our rebellious attitudes and actions. You will find a long *tachanun* and a shorter one in your *siddur*. Learn more about what they are and how and when they are used by seeing the helpful article at Wikipedia.

Sixth Landmark—The Torah Section, is when you read some passage(s) of Scripture as guidance for today's God-honoring choices. This is the pinnacle of the service. All else has been a preparation for this encounter with the word and authority of the King of the Universe, who said to Moses at Sinai, "'You have seen what I did to the Egyptians, and how I carried you on eagles' wings and brought you to myself. Now if you will pay careful attention to what I say and keep my covenant, then you will be my own treasure from among all the peoples, for all the earth is mine; and you will be a kingdom of *cohanim* for me, a nation set apart.' These are the words you are to speak to the people of Isra'el" (Ex 19:4–6, CJB).

Here you would read all or, more likely part, of the Torah reading for the week, the *Haftarah* (prophetic) portion for the week, and the New Covenant portion of the week.[5] Make your own choice. You might even choose another Scripture reading, apart from these traditional reading schedules. Whichever approach you take, find something meaningful to take with you, something to grow on during the day.

Seventh Landmark—Concluding Prayers which help you transition into your day by speaking out some insight you gained from this exercise. Say a prayer, and go meet your day! The chief among these prayers is called *Alenu*, which reminds us that we have a job to do, beginning with the words, "It is our duty." The final thrust of the service is to remind us to cooperate with God, repairing a broken world. This prayer provides our marching orders.[6]

When the service includes a minimum of ten Jews, we may also add the Mourner's *Kaddish* at this point. You might even want to sing the hymns *Adon Olam* or *Ein Kelohenu* which are rousing in character and content. It's a great way to go out into your day!

Helpful Additional Hints:

1. Our people have always placed a high priority on sticking together. This is not hard to understand, considering how for 2,000 years, our ancestors lived as strangers in strange lands, threatened, persecuted, and marginalized. For this reason, even our prayer service reminds us we need each other. Some prayers may only be said when ten Jews of majority age (thirteen years for boys, and more recently, also twelve years for girls) are gathered.[7] For example, without such a quorum,

the *Barchu* just before the *Sh'ma,* and the *Kaddish,* a prayer of praise that pops up punctuating sections of the service, and most memorably, as the Mourner's *Kaddish,* are not said. This acts as a goad to community members that they should attend the services to make sure they do their part to fulfill the quorum.

This communitarian emphasis does *not* mean that we pray in lockstep with everyone else. Jewish prayer services are multi-individual, thus, you keep your individuality, and communitarian, thus you support the group with your participation. How does this work? It's like Jewish jazz. How so?

Keeping track of where the prayer leader is, participants track with the group praying while at the same time respecting their own pace and allowing themselves to pause at times to ponder something that catches their attention. They will do this, honoring the certain places in the service where everyone responds together. This is just like improvising in a jazz ensemble where players follow the same structure of melody, chords, tempo, and rhythm, yet improvise and "do their own thing." Jewish liturgical prayer at its best is "Jewish jazz" or "ensemble praying." When it's done well, it's a blast, or as someone I know says, "It's rad!"

2. Pay attention to body language. Gradually you will learn when it is traditional to stand and learn to make that a habit; also, when to bow, etc. It is true that the Psalmist says, "Bless the LORD, O my soul, and all that is *within* me bless His holy Name" (Ps 103:1, KJV),

but Jewish prayer is not just something interior, simply in the mind, the mouth, and the heart. If you have seen religious Jews praying, you will often see them moving around a bit, and certainly standing and sitting at the appropriate times. The standard Jewish explanation is that this incorporation of the entire body is what David spoke of when he said, "All my bones will say, "Who is like you?" (Ps 35:10, CJB).

3. Changing the metaphor from a jazz ensemble, you might also think of the *siddur* and the conventions of Jewish prayer to be like the text of a play, complete with stage directions. And just as actors are themselves affected and transformed through acting out their parts in their scripts, so are we transformed by "performing" Jewish prayer. These prayers, read aloud, imprint themselves on us, and yes, that's a good thing.

4. Knowing the right melodies makes things more fun. When praying alone, I find it helps to improvise my own chants and motifs. (Of course, this won't work as well when praying in public. And to be honest, it may work easily for me because I am a musician.) Whatever the case, don't get hung up. Don't let your time of prayer become an occasion for rating yourself on how well or how poorly you are doing. This is a time to seek God, using the script of this great play (in which God is the director and star actor!), or the chart of this great inter-generational songbook. Ignore the badgering voices of "experts" who are only concerned to correct you. Look instead for people who want to assist you by answer-

ing and anticipating your questions. Just make sure you enjoy yourself and make it real!

5. Paul, in speaking of his own prayer life, speaks of praying in the Spirit, "For if I pray in a tongue, my spirit does pray, but my mind is unproductive. So, what about it? I will pray with my spirit, but I will also pray with my mind; I will sing with my spirit, but I will also sing with my mind" (1 Cor 14:14–15, CJB).

Some people, as part of their prayer practice, pray in tongues, a transrational kind of vocalization which arises from their spirit, their inner core, which is bonded with the *Ruach HaKodesh*, God's Spirit, who indwells and penetrates into our inner core through our Yeshua-faith. As the Bible underscores, people often find that while having the urge to pray, they cannot find the words, or that their ardor spills over the limitations of their customary articulations (see Ro 8:26). Even when our spirits and minds are soaring in liturgical prayer, this happens for some, who slip over into this syllabic improvisation.

Contrary to what some imagine, this practice is not useless nonsense, but rather, "The one who speaks in a tongue builds himself up" (1 Cor 14:4, NET). Paul even says, "I thank God that I speak in tongues more than all of you" (1 Cor 14:18, NET). So, even if you are not sure this is for you, clearly this form of prayer should not be disparaged. It can well be combined with liturgical prayer, and in a group. If done nondisruptively, praying within oneself and for God alone to hear, one can pray in this manner. Remember, there are "all kinds of prayers and requests, in the Spirit" as Paul wrote to the Ephesians (Eph 6:18, CJB). This is certainly included.

FOR BETTER DIGESTION

1. We said that praying is spending time with our Father and our King, God himself. How do you think your relationship with your own father influences your concept of God and your expectations of him?

2. We discussed both structured approaches to prayer like liturgical prayer, and less structured approaches to prayer like *hitbodedut*. What value do you see in each kind of prayer? Which do you prefer?

3. Which type of prayer in this chapter most appeals to you? How and when do you plan to implement that approach to prayer?

4. Which type of prayer in this chapter least appeals to you? What might you do to expose yourself to that approach and experiment with it?

5. Paul encouraged the Ephesians to practice "all kinds of prayer." Do you think multi-style prayer is a good idea? Why? Why not?

MORE FOOD FOR THOUGHT

(For complete publication information, please see the For Further Reading section.)

On Extemporaneous Prayer

Richard Foster, *Prayer: Finding the Heart's True Home*
This introduction to various styles of prayer by a modern Quaker author with an ecumenical heart is not good for nitpickers who will protest anything that sounds too Catholic. But it is excellent for those looking to identify a style of prayer suitable for themselves.

Albert Haase, *Becoming an Ordinary Mystic: Spirituality for the Rest of Us*
This excellent book is by a Franciscan friar. For those of you suffering from "But is it Catholic?" anxiety, I assure you the book will warm the cockles of your Protestant Evangelical or Messianic Jewish heart. The man is broadly biblical, and the book is even published by InterVarsity Press, a bastion of Evangelical rectitude. The book is practical, very well-written, deeply insightful, and peppered with accounts of real people and real struggles to better know a very real God.

Paul E. Miller, *Beginning a Praying Life*
The author is a pastor and a compassionate expert on prayer who humanizes the process and makes it doable. Much of his prayer life involves praying for a daughter with special needs. This 64-page booklet is a taste of insights from his fine book, *A Praying Life*.

Paul E. Miller, *A Praying Life: Connecting with God in a Distracting World*

This excellent book on prayer will warm you up to how much you need to pray. It deals predominantly with petitionary prayer and intercessory prayer.

Bonnie Thurston, *For God Alone: A Primer on Prayer*

This is a mature book by a thorough scholar with a poet's heart. The book is deep, and repeatedly I found myself underlining because the language is so precise and penetrating, without ever being pretentious. This is not for beginners.

On Rebbe Nachman of Bratslav (Breslov)

Arthur Green, *Tormented Master: The Life and Spiritual Quest of Rabbi Nahman of Bratslav*

This is a respectful and honest biographical retrospective on Rebbe Nachman that gives one reason to believe that he was manic-depressive, although, like others, a genius. Many works based on quotations from the Rebbe may be found on Amazon, and some of those quotes show him to have at times spoken of himself as a Messiah figure. Of course, with this I cannot agree. However, his insights about *hitbodedut* remain brilliant and insightful because lifting despairing souls was (naturally) a preoccupation of his.

Avraham Greenbaum, *Under the Table & How to Get Up: Jewish Pathways of Spiritual Growth*

Rebbe Nachman habitually taught using parables and fables. This is one of them, which will give you occasion to admire his genius. The book includes a well-expressed description of *hitbodedut* and is worth the purchase price for that reason alone.

On Liturgical Prayer

"Prayer: Introduction—Why pray in a traditional Jewish manner?"

From the Messianic Jewish Rabbinical Council, this presents halachically responsible standards for prayer practice. This is good material for people who like well-considered guidelines but may be irksome for people who find guidelines confining and intrusive.

https://ourrabbis.org/main/halakhah-main-menu-26/community-practices/prayer-mainmenu-36

Hayim Halevy Donin, *To Pray as a Jew: A Guide to the Prayer Book and the Synagogue Service*

This is a standard work, comprehensive, and from an Orthodox perspective. I found it a bit stodgy, but your mileage may vary.

Evelyn Garfiel, *Service of the Heart: A Guide to the Jewish Prayer Book*

This book is vastly overpriced right now on Amazon, so pick up a used copy! It is a standard, accessible introduction to the *Siddur*.

Lawrence A. Hoffman, *The Art of Public Prayer: Not for Clergy Only*

This is not a how-to book but rather a series of well-informed essays on the psychology of Jewish prayer and how Jewish services may be conceived of and carried out in the most aesthetically appropriate manner. It is a good book for service designers.

Arnold S. Rosenberg, *Jewish Liturgy as a Spiritual System: A Prayer-by-Prayer Explanation of the Nature and Meaning of Jewish Worship*

This is a brilliant book by a lawyer who loves Jewish life and Jewish prayer. He describes the structure and rationale of the Jewish prayer service, seeing it as a vehicle for consciousness shaping, preparing us to go forth into the world as servants of *HaShem*. Well worth the purchase price and fascinating.

Jordan Lee Wagner, *The Synagogue Survival Kit: A Guide to Understanding Jewish Religious Services*

This ultimate user-friendly guide to everything involved in the synagogue service and in synagogue behaviors is very user-friendly. Shop around for a copy you can afford.

On *Siddurim*

Choosing a *siddur* is a developmental, personal, and communal process. At different stages in our lives, each of us will favor one or the other. Most of us who engage in Jewish communal prayer have more than one we like to use. *Siddurim* differ in the communal traditions they serve, in the texts they include, in their translations, in their layouts, in the presence or absence of transliteration, and in the ways in which their editors seek to assist us with the work of prayer.

I am grateful to Rabbi Yahnatan Lasko, Rabbi Joshua Brumbach, Rabbi Paul Saal, Rabbi David Wein, and David Nichol for their informed recommendations on these matters.

Of Orthodox *siddurim*, they recommended the *Koren Sacks Siddur, Koren Talpiot Siddur, Koren Rav Kook Siddur*, and *Artscroll Siddur*.

Of Conservative *siddurim*, both *Sim Shalom*, and *Lev Shalem* got high marks. *Kol Haneshamah* (Reconstructionist) is also well worth considering.

Daniel Pressman and Ronald Isaacs, *Siddur Or Shalom Le-Shabat Ve-Yom Tov (Siddur Or Shalom for Shabbat and Festivals)*

This fully transliterated *siddur* for Shabbat and festivals, compatible with the *Siddur Sim Shalom* of the Conservative Movement, is outrageously inexpensive!

For a Reform *Siddur*, see *Mishkan T'filah*.

https://ccarpress.org/shopping_product_detail. asp?pid=50203

Koren Prayerbooks

This publisher is noted for the beauty of its typography and layout, its sophisticated translations, and erudite commentary, especially that done by Rabbi Jonathan Sacks, of Blessed Memory.

https://korenpub.com/collections/siddurim

Conservative Prayerbooks

The *Sim Shalom Siddur* is user-friendly, attractive, and somewhat contemporary. In recent years the Conservative Movement has also produced the *Siddur Lev Shalem*. Read about both of them here, and also about other liturgical resources.

https://www.rabbinicalassembly.org/resources-ideas/publications/prayerbooks

On Messianic Jewish *Siddurim*

John Fisher and David Bronstein, *Sidur li-Yehudim Meshihim (Siddur for Messianic Jews)*

This is one of the very earliest efforts in this area. The services are somewhat abbreviated. Unfortunately, the price on Amazon is prohibitive.

Barry Budoff, *A Messianic Jewish Siddur for Shabbat, in Hebrew and English*

This *siddur* endeavors to be somewhat complete and as of this writing is out of print, although it may again become available.

Isaac S. Roussel, *Shabbat Siddur: Siddur Zera Avraham*

This *siddur* and related liturgical materials are excellent integrations of respectful use of traditional sources combined with unforced and appropriate integration of Messianic Jewish faith and practice. The layout is user-friendly, the translations elegant, and the price is unbelievably low. However, be prepared for small print.

Here are a few websites to assist you in comparison shopping for *siddurim* (prayerbooks) not only for weekdays but also for Shabbat, as well as prayerbooks for other occasions. I encourage you to consult with trusted mentors who know you and your community to help guide you in the choices you will make.

Choose Your *Siddur*

This is a good article about comparing *siddurim* and the wide variety of *siddurim* out there for your consideration.

https://www.myjewishlearning.com/article/how-to-choose-a-siddur/

TAKE-OUT

Remember this! Yeshua taught his disciples always to pray and not give up (Luke 18:1). Let that be you!

CHAPTER TWO

MAKING A *MOTZI*: THE BREAD OF THE WORD

Having opened this holy meal with a *kiddush* in the prior chapter, we follow up by beginning this chapter with a taste of bread, which we call a *motzi*. As you no doubt know, religious Jews ordinarily begin a meal by saying a blessing over bread, a process termed *making a motzi*. In fact, in Jewish life, a meal is not a meal unless there is bread.

The Bible is also big on bread, using it as a metaphor for what is central to our spiritual life. Both Moshe (Moses) and Yeshua (Jesus) compare God's words to bread, reminding us "man does not live by bread alone, but by every word that proceeds from the mouth of God." So, what's the point? Just as there is no meal unless bread is eaten, so there is no spiritual feast without the word of God. In fact, it is *such* a feast that it is compared not only to bread, but also to milk and to meat!

This is why the Bible is a basic food group for people who want to be spiritually robust. When we eat the words of Scripture, whether by reading, study, or discussion, God meets us in the process, as long as we don't turn the journey into an ego trip.

Maybe your experience mirrors mine. When I meet people in the Jewish and Christian context who have a certain spiritual gravitas, I generally discover that they make a habit of engaging with Scripture. Such people radiate stability and sobriety mixed with a kind of holy gladness.

Maybe you think you don't have time for this. Maybe you sense that the learning curve is steep, and you're not sure you want to bother. I can relate. And to be honest, like any other habit, serious engagement with Scripture *will* take time. But not as much as you'd expect. And the good news is this: Your appetite for Scripture will grow with each nourishing meal. It gets easier, and you'll quickly become what I am—a big advocate for the practice.

So here's the point: Make a habit of eating the bread of the Word and you will grow in gravitas. But how?

Ways to Eat the Bread of the Word

It's nice to have choices, so let's look at three ways to eat the bread of the Word—the Horner Method, the Hendricks Method, and the *Havruta* Method. Each successive method takes you deeper into your engagement with Scripture, so you may find yourself sticking to an earlier method until your Scripture reading appetite grows. Then you'll move on to investigating one of the other methods. All of this is good!

Spoiler alert: This chapter gives only a summary of each of these methods, like an appetizer. Supporting details and tips appear in Chapter Twelve to accompany and encourage you on your journey. Bible scholar and teacher Walter C. Kaiser, Jr. calls such details "cookies on the top shelf." By this he means materials requiring you to stretch yourself a bit if you want to get hold of them. We'll be putting these details in Chapter Twelve where you can reach for them if you wish!

Let's look at the Horner Method first.

The Horner Method

Grant Horner is an avid film critic and world-class rock climber. He is also Professor of Renaissance Reformation Studies at The Master's University in Sun Valley, California. He's never gone to Bible school or seminary. Still, he has a prodigious knowledge of Scripture. He even remembers where texts are on the page, without having to open the book to find out. All of us can reach this level, and Horner shows us how.

To use the Horner Method, create ten bookmarks, using some sort of stiff paper, perhaps what is known as "card stock." If you really want to be fancy after creating the bookmarks, laminate them and they will never wear out. On each bookmark, write a short list of Bible books, in the process covering all the books of the Bible distributed among the bookmarks. For example, the first bookmark could have Genesis, Exodus, Leviticus, Numbers, and Deuteronomy (the five books of the Torah). Then do the same with another set of books—perhaps Joshua, Judges, Ruth, First and Second Samuel.

Continue this process until all the books of the Bible are distributed among the ten bookmarks, listing more books per bookmark when some are short and fewer books per bookmark when some are long. I adapted the practice so that all the books of the Bible are covered in nine bookmarks. I reserve the tenth bookmark for books of the Bible that I especially want to master. This means that the names of these books will appear on this tenth bookmark and on other bookmarks as well. In this way, these books will get double duty.

So what do we do with all these bookmarks? Easy. For starters, place each bookmark at the beginning of the first book listed on that bookmark. So, place the first bookmark at Genesis, Chapter 1, and the second bookmark at Joshua, Chapter 1, etc.

Once all of this is set up, you would read the first chapter of the first book on each bookmark the first day, and the second chapter for that same first book on each bookmark the second day. And when you finish the first book on each bookmark, you would then go on to the second book on each bookmark and do the same thing. And when you finish all the books on a bookmark, you start all over again.

Yes, this means reading ten chapters a day, one for each bookmark. It sounds like a lot, but after you get the hang of things, it will take about 45 minutes. Follow this method, and you will read the Bible through three times a year. And because each bookmark has a different number of chapters on it, you will never be reading the same ten chapters together on another day.

You will find my example of these ten bookmarks graphically displayed in the Appendix. It shows one way to organize your bookmarks, but I encourage you to dream up your own recipe, too. There are other examples available online by searching "Images for Horner bookmarks."

Here are some ways to make this method your own and to build in enough flexibility to help it fit into the ebb and flow of your life:

1. Sometimes you may want to spend your time differently, concentrating on reading further in just one or two books that day, for instance. That will mean you are not going to hit every bookmark that day. This is *fine!* This flexibility will keep you engaged for the long haul. So *do* be flexible in how you use the method. But use the "ten chapters from ten different places" approach as your base. Ultimately, it will yield the best results.

2. If you miss a day, don't punish yourself by requiring yourself to do twice as many chapters the next day. Doing that will destroy your motivation. If you miss a day or more, just get back on the bicycle and start peddling from where you are.

3. Use the same edition of the same Bible each day, year after year, and when that Bible wears out, get a duplicate. This will work toward enabling you to picture where on the page your texts are when you recall them to mind. Yes, really, your mind will work that way.

4. If reading ten chapters at a time seems impractical for you, you may want to read five chapters in the morning and five chapters later in the day.

5. Don't slow yourself down by looking up cross-references or taking copious notes. The purpose of this approach is breadth, not depth, to give you an overview of the Bible. So, keep moving! But I will confess that I often jot something down from the day's reading that especially applies to my life. But don't overdo this.

Using the Horner Method, you will discover interconnections in the Bible every day that you never saw before, and you will also come across truths directly applicable to your life. Trust me on this: It's a transformational experience.

The Hendricks Method: Going Deeper

Howard Hendricks was a legendary professor of the Bible who insisted that the measure of a teacher's excellence was how well his students learned. By that measure, Hendricks was a genius. He taught thousands of Bible students who became excellent Bible teachers themselves.

Stuart Dauermann

Like any really good teacher, Hendricks (known as "Prof" to his students) impressed everyone by making the complicated easy to understand. He spoke of *four steps in Bible study*. To these four I have added six more that expand upon his insights. Rather than think of these as ten steps in Bible study, I prefer to think of these as ten aspects of Bible study which we should keep in mind if we want to draw reliable conclusions from what we read there.

In contrast to the Horner Method, which focuses on what the Bible says, Hendricks focuses on what the Bible *means* by what it says. Some people imagine the Bible's meaning is explicit, and we need no help understanding it. Perhaps you have heard the slogan, "The Bible says it, I believe it, and that settles it." Well, not exactly. No one ever reads the Bible without interpreting it, and that's where we can either get into trouble, or into truth.

Every day, people draw wrong conclusions from what they read in the Bible. We need some principles to help us form valid and defensible interpretations of what we read there. The Hendricks Method comes to our rescue.

Explaining the Hendricks Method

Hendricks's four basic steps are:

1. Observe the evidence of the text.

53

2. Interpret what that evidence meant to its original author and audience.

3. Apply that meaning to your own situation.

4. Capture and communicate the impact of this Bible passage for the benefit of others.

Stated in this way, these aspects of Bible study are very broad. But of course, in teaching these aspects, Hendricks provided a detailed roadmap to getting things done. The six steps I add are, for the most part, the kinds of details Hendricks provides when he fleshes out his four basic steps. This makes a total of ten steps that are really aspects or mentalities for effectively reading and interpreting the Bible:

1. Prayerfully rely upon the *Ruach*, the Divine Presence.

2. Always ask the Jewish Bible study question—Why does the text say it *this* way and not another?

3. Use your faculties of reason.

4. Observe the evidence of the text.

5. Interpret what that evidence meant to its original author and audience.

6. Double-check your understanding with at least two translations besides the one you normally use. And if you understand the original language of the text, Hebrew or Greek, so much the better!

7. Meditate on the text to sense its significance for your own life and situation.

8. Process all of this within the Jewish tradition and in consultation with the best insights of the Christian world.

9. Apply the meaning of the text to your own situation.

10. Capture and communicate the impact of this Bible passage for the benefit of others.

Let's deal with the first four items here, and transfer the rest of our amplification of the Hendricks Method to the end of this book in Chapter Twelve, "Cookies on the Top Shelf." As mentioned, Walter C. Kaiser's metaphor refers to delicious information you have to stretch yourself to obtain. Not everyone will make the effort, but if you want to go get it, the "cookies" are on the top shelf in Chapter Twelve.

Step One: Prayerfully rely upon the Ruach, the Divine Presence.

Studying Scripture is not simply an academic enterprise; it is also meant to be an avenue of spiritual encounter. Therefore, we should always study with a prayerful reliance upon the Divine Presence. You can do this simply. Begin your study of Scripture by asking God for his help in your understanding of it. My standard prayer in all kinds of situations is very simple. It's "Help me, Father." Often it's "Help me, help me, help me!" And I mean it!

Or you might use this blessing from our Jewish tradition, "*Baruch atah* ADONAI, *Eloheinu Melech ha-olam, asher kid'shanu b'mitzvotav, v'tzivanu la'asok b'divre Torah,*" ("Blessed are You, our LORD our God, King of the Universe, who has set us apart by his commandments, and commanded us to occupy ourselves with the words of Torah [Holy Instruction].") This blessing may be used for studying any part of the Bible. However we may elevate our consciousness at this time, our goal is not to be mindless in our study of holy things, but to maintain a sense of dependency on the Divine Presence.

Step Two: Always ask the Jewish Bible study question—Why does the text say it this way and not another?

Traditionally, Jews regard the text of Scripture as holy. Every detail of the text is significant. This respect for detail has bred millennia of careful, attentive, and life-changing study. Jews are interested not only in what the text says, but also in why things are said in a certain way. For example, why is a story retold in the Bible with certain details added or missing? Why is the text precisely as it is?

And while this approach to the text applies to the original languages more than to any translation, still, this mentality of attentiveness to detail will serve us well in whatever language we read the Bible. Asking why the text says things the way it does, and why parallel accounts differ, serves as a goad toward attentiveness. Since textual details matter, it will be a good idea to frequently consult a Bible that follows a word-for-word translational approach.

There are basically two kinds of Bible translations. Word-for-word (also known as formal equivalence) translations try to match the original language words with the closest English language counterpart. The New American Standard translation is a favorite in this regard. Another kind of translation, following a different translational philosophy, is a thought-for-thought (dynamic equivalence) translation that seeks to produce in the reader an impact as close as possible to the assumed impact the text had on its original hearers in the original languages (Greek, Aramaic, and Hebrew). In such translations, creating equivalent ideas and impact (rather than simply equivalent words) is the focus.

Most serious students of Scripture will consult and read a variety of translations from time to time and from situation to situation. Inevitably, since people are different, each of us will find some translation as our favorite, our go-to version. Even so, when studying, having a word-for-word kind of translation nearby is helpful for details, just as some other version may prove helpful for readability. It is helpful also to use Jewish translations as well, both from the wider Jewish community and from the Messianic Jewish world. For those who are able, reading in the original languages is always in order.

Step Three: Use your faculties of reason.

Studying the Bible is not a touchy-feely, sub-intellectual or anti-intellectual pursuit. On the contrary, it demands the best that is in us, including our intellectual capacities and our most astute discernment. We should bring to the Bible the kind of intense focus brought by a detective or a forensic examiner analyzing a crime scene. Attention counts because details count.

The story is told about Saul of Tarsus, aka the Apostle Paul, who had to leave Thessalonica (in Greece) because some people in the local synagogue drove him out of town. So, Paul and his entourage made their way to Berea, a small city nearby. Notice what the text says about how the Bereans responded to Paul:

> Now the Berean Jews were of more noble
> character than those in Thessalonica, for
> they received the message with great
> eagerness and examined the Scriptures
> every day to see if what Paul said was true.
> (Acts 17:11, NIV)

What made the Bereans "of more noble character" than their neighbors in Thessalonica wasn't just their hospitality. It was also how they cared enough about the truth to diligently check things out as they "examined the Scriptures every day to see if what Paul said was true." The Greek root behind the term "examined" in this text is *anakrino*, and it means to investigate, interrogate, or examine in such a manner as a judge would conduct an investigation. *This* is the way we are to study the Bible. Not touchy-feely, but carefully and analytically.

Reading the Bible *can* be boring, but not if you bring your best game. We have to be alert and attentive, always asking ourselves, "Does what I am seeing and what I am concluding make sense? Am I missing something? Am I reading something into this that just isn't there?" Reading Scripture lights up for us when we strike the balance the Bereans struck: Receive the word gladly, but check things out to make sure they are true.

And here's a hint that changes everything: People in the Bible operated with a different worldview than we do. The questions they asked and answered, their sense of their place in the scheme of things, their assessment of the meaning of life, their assumptions about the interfacing of spiritual and material reality were mostly different from our own assumptions. This does not make their views primitive or noncredible. Some of the greatest geniuses of Western civilization treated the Bible as unique, authoritative, and God-breathed. While reading the Bible requires that we bring our best game and our highest rationality, it also demands we become aware of how our own assumptions can both determine and distort what we see and think.

René Descartes famously said, "I think, therefore I am," establishing the perceiving self at the center of reality. But consider this: If the Bible is true, then there is Someone else at the center of reality besides you or me. Instead of reading Scripture in the shadow of Descartes's "I think, therefore I am," we should read it in the shadow of Moses, in the light of the Burning Bush, attentive to the One who said, "I am that I am." How might your worldview shift if you entertained the possibility that the God of our ancestors is the source of all beingness?

By all means, use your powers of reason. But as Jewish tradition wisely advises us all, "Know before whom you stand." It's not René Descartes!

Step Four: Observe the evidence of the text.

Here we ask and answer the question, "What do I see here?" I know this seems so obvious—you just read the text and if your eyes are good, that's it! Good luck with that! It's better to agree with George Orwell who said, "To see what's in front of your nose requires a constant struggle."[1] Sherlock Holmes put it this way in *The Hound of the Baskervilles:* "The world is full of obvious things which nobody by any chance ever observes."[2] Imagining that things are obvious contributes to inattentional blindness. Instead, imagine there is more here than meets the eye. Don't jump to conclusions. Collect details.

Orwell and Holmes are talking about "inattention-al blindness." This concept came to the attention of the public through a famous video[3] by Christopher Chabris and Daniel Simons in which a group of six young people, three in white shirts, three in black, are milling about, passing around basketballs to others on their team. Viewers of the video are directed to count how many times the white team passes the ball. After viewers report on their counts, they are asked, "Did you see the gorilla?"

"What? What gorilla?" In the midst of the video, someone dressed in a gorilla suit walks slowly onto the screen from the right side, stops and waves at the viewer, and walks off to the left side. If you haven't heard the statistics before, you will be astounded to discover that in general, about 50–60% of viewers never see the gorilla! This is "inattentional blindness,"[4] not seeing something, even something obvious, because you are busy paying attention elsewhere. There are things that we miss, things as big as a gorilla, because our minds are preoccupied with other matters.

To avoid wasting our time and missing the action, we need to avoid inattentional blindness when reading the text of Scripture. But how? Read on.

Slow down and ask the right questions: To avoid missing what others might miss, learn to *slow down.* One of the best ways to do this is to ask the questions journalism students learn on Day One: who, what, when, where, why, and how. Forming the habit of interrogating the text (like those Bereans did and as journalists do) will slow us down and bring things into focus that we might otherwise ignore or assume we already know.

- *Who questions:* Who wrote the text, and, in the case of letters, who received them? Who is being discussed?
- *What questions:* What is going on in the text? What just happened? What is about to happen? What situations are we looking at? What seems to be the problem?
- *When questions:* When was this written? What do we know about the events of that time period?
- *Where questions:* Where was this written? How does the culture of that location affect the content of the text?
- *Why questions:* Why was this written? Can we spot the underlying purpose or point of this text?
- *How questions:* How was this writing discovered and preserved? What can we discover about the history of this text?

Notice emphasis and repetition: You can generally assume that when a biblical author repeats a theme or an idea, it means that idea or theme is important to the point he is making. Therefore, slow down and look for repetitions and other forms of emphasis. These are keys to where the evidence of the text is pointing.

Identify key words and phrases: Repeated readings of a text (strongly recommended!) will give you a feeling for the issues driving the author, what problems he is addressing, and what he is getting at. Sometimes a repeated concept will be labeled using the same term, but often the vocabulary is varied, using synonyms. To identify key words and concepts, ask yourself, "What seems to be ringing the author's chimes?" Believe me, this is fascinating stuff, and you can't get it by doing a Google search! The fun is in hunkering down and noticing what others miss. It's right there, but you'll be repeatedly amazed that others don't see what you see.

Notice comparisons and contrasts: While all the books of the Bible make frequent use of comparison and contrast, one genre—wisdom literature—specializes in it. Whenever the text of Scripture begins to explain or to teach, comparisons (how things are alike) and contrasts (how they differ) abound.

"The LORD is my shepherd; I shall not want." (How is the LORD my shepherd?)

"You are the light of the world!" (How are we the light of the world?)

"He (the person who meditates on God's Torah) shall be like a tree planted by streams of water." (How?)

"At one time you were darkness, but now you are light in the Lord. Walk as children of light." (How were we in darkness; how can we walk as children of light?)

"Go in through the narrow gate; for the gate that leads to destruction is wide and the road broad, and many travel it; but it is a narrow gate and a hard road that leads to life, and only a few find it." (What is the narrow gate? What is the wide gate? What characterizes people who choose one or the other? Why do people make these choices? How can we know which gate we are choosing?)

You might be surprised to know that most people never ask these kinds of questions. When we assume matters are obvious, we are almost certain to miss what we ought to notice. Don't be that person! And when you have difficulty answering your questions, the best place to look for clarification will be the immediate context and then the wider context of the passage you are considering.

Be attentive to genre: Genre refers to the type of text we are dealing with. In general, you will find seven different genres in Scripture, and each one alerts us to needed perspectives and principles for how to rightly understand the meaning of the text. Don't let this intimidate you. You're already familiar with most of this from your own observations. Here's a quick glance at the seven genres:

1. **Narrative**—Tells stories to emphasize lessons the author wants us to learn.

2. **Wisdom literature**—Tells the way life works from the vantage point of a sage within the community. This kind of literature specializes in comparisons and contrasts.

3. **Poetry**—Uses imaginative metaphors and ways of organizing lines to stress parallels and contrasts. Po-

etry tends to be emotional, expressing the subjective aspects of living as God's people in an often challenging and dangerous world.

4. **Prophecy**—Just as narrative texts tell stories, so prophecy is like newspaper opinion pieces about the meaning and outcome of those events. If narrative is the front page of a newspaper, prophecy is the editorial page or opinion page.

5. **Gospels**—These are not just biographies of Yeshua but are narrations of his story from incarnation to consummation, lighting the way for how we ought to live our lives.

6. **Epistles**—These are "occasional letters" written to respond to and address historical situations in the lives of some of the earliest communities of Yeshua-believers. They are not theological treatises, although they can get quite theological. They are meant to address actual problems and situations. Therefore, to rightly interpret such letters, the enjoyable and challenging task is to detect clues in the text that help us identify what those problems or situations were, what solutions or perspectives were being offered, and ways in which the problems, solutions, or both are parallel to situations we face in our own lives.

7. **Apocalyptic writing**—These are like the political cartoons in the newspaper. They include exaggerated word pictures designed to make truths vivid. Just as political cartoons use elephants to represent the Republican Party and donkeys to represent the Democratic

Party, apocalyptic literature uses animals and various objects from nature and daily life to represent nations, events, and peoples. Because of its highly symbolic character, we must avoid being too literal in interpreting apocalyptic literature. We should always be asking, "What does this stand for, and how do I know that to be the case? What perspectives, events, or spiritual realities are being represented here?" And most important, "How is my situation parallel to what I see here, and how does this document shed light on my own situation, if at all?"

If you are hungry for more details on the Hendricks Method, don't miss the "cookies" in Chapter Twelve.

The *Havruta* Method

The *Havruta* Method is our third method of Bible study with a long history in Jewish life. This partnering method of interacting with Scripture will really get your juices flowing!

Havruta study employs established mechanisms for rigorously interacting with holy texts along with active study partners, each of whom is also termed a *havruta*.[5] The term, sometimes spelled *hevruta*, or *chavrusa*, is related to the word "*haver*," meaning brother, and the word "*hevra*" meaning friendship, companionship, or "fellowship." We study with such partners because all of us have blind spots, and in study, as in so much of life, we will get by with a little help from our friends.

Here's a formal definition: A *havruta* is a learning partnership, usually between two parties, sometimes three or maybe even four, who, through an iron-sharpening-iron process, enhance their mutual learning in ways not otherwise possible, while valuing both disagreement and discovery. This dialectical approach to learning is done aloud with one's *havruta* partner(s).

This is a relational approach to learning. Religious Jews may study with the same learning partner for years, even decades, and the personal history the partners share with each other deeply impacts their experience over time. Such partners will find that their own perspective on the text has been imprinted by the personality and insights of their partner. In this manner, not only the text, but also our partners, become part of us.

The *havruta* philosophy insists that one simply cannot learn by oneself as deeply or richly as when learning with someone else. This is so for many reasons—our own laziness, blind spots, academic limitations, and tendency to project our own meanings onto texts and even to hide from insights we prefer to avoid. *Havruta* study forces us to be honest and objective.

Also, we will go much deeper and learn much better when we explain a text's meaning and implications to others. This method obliges us to defend and justify our position and also to seriously consider and interact with how others see things. We do this through following a rhythm of speaking and listening, observing and reflecting, disagreeing and agreeing.

In the *havruta* method, "the truth is out there." This approach assumes that God reveals meaning not simply to individuals, but to the community, and that we need to hear one another in order to hear the truth God means for us to know. We accomplish this hearing through our encounter with the text and with each other. This should remind us of Paul's word to the prophets in Corinth, "Let two or three prophets speak, and let the others weigh what is said" (1 Cor 14:29, CJB). It is not just the speaking of the prophets that unveils truth; it is the deliberations of the community weighing what they have heard. In *havruta* study, the text is another partner in the discussion, and we must weigh what it says with the assistance of others.

Orit Kent explores the rhythms of *havruta* study in "A Theory of *Havruta* Learning,"[6] summarizing the dynamics of *havruta* learning as three pairs of core practices: listening and articulating, wondering and focusing, and supporting and challenging.[7] The interaction of these pairs, held in dynamic tension, makes texts come alive in new ways. Let's look at them more closely.

First pair: Listening and articulating

"Listening" means that both learning partners must pay attention to the text as they read it aloud to each other and must also listen to one another as they share and justify their interpretations of the meaning and applications of the text. Hearing and listening are not the same thing. One can hear without really listening, and we must listen deeply to each other in order to fan the flames of understanding.

"Articulating," the necessary companion to listening, means "expressing one's ideas out loud."[8] Passivity is not permitted in this learning model. Each partner must make the effort to ensure their interpretations and opinions are explicitly understood.

Second pair: Wondering and focusing

"Wondering" reminds us that partners must be prepared to try ideas on for size, to use their imaginations as they seek to vitally interact with each other and the text, unearthing the meaning and import of what they are considering. By doing so, they stretch the boundaries of how they normally see things and get beyond the obvious. In other words, both learning partners must risk getting "outside the box." Jewish study values bringing our imaginations into the interpretive process, as for example, trying to imagine the backstory of what is on the page. It is by such wondering that the text comes alive to us as the record of lived human experience related to our own.

"Focusing" is the companion to wondering. It entails "concentrating attention in order to deepen an interpretation and come to some conclusion about the meaning of the text."[9] If wondering may be compared to daydreaming, then focusing is "just the facts, Ma'am."

Third pair: Supporting and challenging

"Supporting means providing encouragement for the ideas on the table, encouraging and helping proponents to clarify their observations, making them stronger though marshalling evidence."[10] Here is where each study partner encourages the other to explain what he or she sees in the text, and why.

Its companion discipline, "challenging," consists of raising problems with the viewpoint being advocated, suggesting missing elements, and drawing attention to contradictions and better alternatives.[11]

How Is Havruta Study Implemented?

The way one does *havruta* study is rather simple, but profound:

- You sit down with your study partner(s), perhaps two or three, but no more.
- You pray, giving thanks to God for his word, asking for his help in your studies, acknowledging you are coming together to fulfill the responsibility of studying his word for its own sake, what our tradition calls "*Talmud Torah lishma*," meaning, "study of the Torah for its name."

70

- Then, out loud, you and your study partner(s) go through the process together, even freely using approaches described under the Hendricks method, and doing it aloud. But again, this is not a solo process but is one with partners, actualizing the three pairs of dynamics we just described: listening and articulating, wondering and focusing, and supporting and challenging.

- It is especially valuable to bring into the discussion information about how your communal tradition views these matters. In Jewish study, this means the sages, scholars, and leaders of the Jewish people. In this way, these persons participate in your discussion. But always, the text is king.

- You will be amazed at how the text will come alive to you in new ways, and how you and your study partner(s) will come away from the experience with a new understanding of the text and its implications. You will know you have been truly successful if you come away with questions you never had before. This kind of Jewish study is not so much about finding answers as it is discovering the important questions the text is asking us concerning how we think and live.

To Summarize

We've looked together at three ways to eat and drink the milk, the meat, and the bread of the Word.

• The Horner Method gives us a dependable and interactive overview of the entire Bible. Think of this as the multiple vitamins of your spiritual life, giving you a necessary foundation for spiritual strength and vitality.

• The Hendricks Method provides basic skills for ramping up our attention as we study texts. This is a method which enables us to interrogate and examine the text as the evidence God has left us of what he wants us to know and consider. We come to the text like Sherlock Holmes, armed with core perspectives and questions that will help us as never before to see what's in front of our noses. All of this forms a basis for discovering the meaning of the text for its original hearers, and its relevance to our lives.

• The *Havruta* Method is where we knock things up a notch further, involving others in our adventurous examination of the text. With one, two, or three study partners, we look at the text, employing tools provided by Hendricks, enhanced by the dynamics of listening and articulating, wondering and focusing, and supporting and challenging. When each partner is being conscientious in this process, the text will leap into life right before our eyes, enlivening our understanding and illumining our lives. The text moves from the page into our minds, hearts, and lives. As with so much in our relationship with God, we've got to "taste and see."

FOR BETTER DIGESTION

1. The most basic question to ask ourselves about reading and studying the Bible is, "Why bother?" How would you answer that question?

2. Is taking a methodological approach to the Bible unnecessary? Shouldn't we just pick it up and see what we get out of it?

3. How does the cultural and chronological distance between us and the people in Biblical times dictate our intellectual effort into interpreting its meaning for ourselves?

4. How has your attitude toward reading the Bible changed as you've become more engaged with Yeshua of Nazareth? Why is that?

5. The *Havruta* Method involves studying with one or two others in an active dialogue framework. Have you found this approach to problem solving or learning to be useful in other aspects of your educational or professional life?

MORE FOOD FOR THOUGHT

(For complete publication information, please see the For Further Reading section.)

The Horner Method

https://sohmer.net/media/professor_grant_horners_bible_reading_system.pdf

The Hendricks Method

https://www.biblestudymagazine.com/bible-study-magazine-blog/2016/7/27/howard-hendricks-4-bible-study-steps

David R. Bauer and Robert A. Traina, *Inductive Bible Study: A Comprehensive Guide to the Practice of Hermeneutics*

The most comprehensive treatment on Inductive Bible Study available. For those of you who like books that are the last word on a subject. Highly technical.

Howard G. Hendricks and William D. Hendricks, *Living by the Book.* Set of 2 books—book and workbook, paperback

User-friendly.

Robert A. Traina, *Methodical Bible Study*

The foundational book upon which inductive Bible study methods are based, such as the Hendricks method. Somewhat technical.

The Havruta Method

Stuart Dauermann, *The Jewish Advantage: What It Is and How to Make It Your Own*
A brief monograph that expands upon *havruta* material covered in this chapter. User-friendly and very helpful.

Elie Holzer and Orit Kent, *A Philosophy of Havruta: Understanding and Teaching the Art of Text Study in Pairs*
Excellent treatment of the subject by experts in the field.

TAKE-OUT

In Matthew 4:4, Yeshua affirms what Torah teaches, that "man does not live by bread alone, but by every word that comes from the mouth of Adonai" (D'varim/ Deuteronomy 8:3, Matthew 4:4, CJB). If Yeshua compared Scripture to nourishment for our bodies, let's make sure we don't starve our souls. Eat His Book, that is, the word of Adonai!

CHAPTER THREE

TASTEFUL TALK

We used to call them "anti-missionaries," members of the Jewish religious community who dedicate themselves to preventing Jews from coming to believe in Yeshua, or who seek to dismantle that faith in new Jewish adherents. One of these wrote an article in a Los Angeles Jewish community tabloid "outing" a prominent leader among Jewish believers in Yeshua, making a big deal over the fact that his mother wasn't a Jew. This was an exercise in public shaming.

In response, I wrote that this man had just committed what Jewish life considers the worst social sin, "*halvanat panim*—whitening of the face," meaning public humiliation. In Jewish life, there is scarcely anything worse you can do.

That's your nosh for this chapter. Judaism extols ethical speech and treats unethical speech as the greatest no-no.

And that reminds me of another story.

He was a retired and distinguished urban businessman. Grey hair, nice clothes, well-groomed. The kind of man who always had to look good for his clientele. Now he was serving as Board Chairman of an agency bringing Yeshua-faith to Jewish people. So maybe it wasn't nice for me to hit him with a verbal 2x4. But sometimes ya gotta do what ya gotta do! And I did!

We were at some meeting, standing together and chatting over a cup of coffee when I said it: "In my opinion, when it comes to speech ethics, Jewish religious culture is superior to Christian religious culture."

He flushed. Confusion wrote its name on his face. He nearly spilled his coffee. He even staggered a bit. Up until then, he had always respected me. But now, here I was, saying that Jewish religious culture was better at something than Christian religious culture. Did he hear me right? I had just transgressed an unquestioned, and even unquestionable, Christian axiom—that all things Christian are an advance over all things Jewish. Doesn't every Yeshua-believer know that Judaism is at best a rough draft for the glories of Christianity?

The answer is, "No." And I stand by what I said. When it comes to speech ethics, Jewish standards and teaching overshadows its Christian counterparts. There's no contest, really.

And if you've ever been disappointed or disgusted with our trash-talk culture, pause here for a while and fortify yourself.

Many religious Jews study Jewish laws of speech every day. This study is grounded in the writings of Rabbi Israel Meir HaKohen Kagan, (1838–1933) who is known as the Chofetz Chaim. His principled conduct and the books he wrote more than a hundred years ago maintain his reputation as the reigning exemplar on the study of *lashon hora* (evil speech), and why and how to avoid it.

The man was a bonafide *tzaddik*, a spiritual giant. Despite acclaim, he elected to remain a poor shopkeeper, more concerned with not cheating his customers than with his profit margin. He wrote 21 authoritative books on standards of Jewish practice, with his first (1873) being *Sefer Chofetz Chaim* (*The Book of the One Who Seeks Life*), the first attempt to organize and clarify Jewish laws about evil talk and gossip. It remains the foundation of all discussion of speech ethics among religious Jews. Later, he wrote *Shmirat HaLashon* (*Guard the Tongue*), which explored what the Sages of Israel taught on speech ethics. It seems impossible to find any aspect of proper and improper speech that is not covered in his works. Remarkable.

Although he wrote more than a century ago, you will find numerous websites devoted to daily study of his works. And so, the question arises, can you name Christian sources that are similarly focused on speech ethics? Probably not. Therefore, my friend shouldn't have been shocked at my statement. He could have learned something, not from me, but from the Jewish world.

People are still making contributions in this area. Messianic Jewish theologian Mark S. Kinzer wrote a tightly-reasoned biblical treatment on speech ethics, *Taming the Tongue.*[1] He reminds us, "The tongue has power over life and death" (Prov 18:21, CJB). The book is a gem, well-written, with no flab. He goes right to the point.

You might also read *Words That Hurt, Words That Heal: How to Choose Words Wisely and Well* by Rabbi Joseph Telushkin.[2] While Kinzer focuses on analyzing Scripture, Telushkin focuses on contemporary illustrations, mostly from news sources, displaying the destructiveness of contemporary *lashon hora*, that is, evil or unethical speech. His stories are stunning. I once taught through this book at my synagogue. We all knew we had been nailed.

THE WHY

I think you will agree, and few would disagree, that contemporary civil discourse is in sharp decline. Whether through sexualized, violent, misogynistic song lyrics; rapid-fire denunciations and characterizations on social media, radio, and TV; or daily political mudslinging; for many, trash-talking is the game to be played. But at what cost?

Any sensitive child will tell you the nursery rhyme was wrong to say, "Sticks and stones many break my bones, but words will never hurt me." In some ways, words do more serious and lasting harm than any stick or stone.

Kinzer reminds us how powerful words are, quoting the psalmist, "By the word of ADONAI the heavens were made, and their whole host by a breath from his mouth" (Ps 33:6, CJB). When the Jewish people were at the base of Mount Sinai, terrified to encounter God, they told Moses, "Speak to us yourself and we will listen; but do not have God speak to us, or we will die!" (Exod 20:19, NASB) They were terrified by the power of the words of ADONAI.

Judaism enshrines the power of words with the iconic declaration, "Hear, O Israel!" The spoken word, rather than images, rules at the center of Jewish religious consciousness. Words are the very stuff from which reality was made. So it's no surprise that Judaism pays so much attention to how human beings, made in the image of God, talk to and about each other.

Kinzer quotes Matthew 12 with a powerful and chilling word from Yeshua of Nazareth about our accountability to God for the words that we speak.

> If you make a tree good, its fruit will be good; and if you make a tree bad, its fruit will be bad; for a tree is known by its fruit. You snakes! How can you who are evil say anything good? For the mouth speaks what overflows from the heart. The good person brings forth good things from his store of good, and the evil person brings forth evil things from his store of evil.

81

Moreover, I tell you this: on the Day of Judgment people will have to give account for every careless word they have spoken; for by your own words you will be acquitted, and by your own words you will be condemned. (Mt 12:33–37, CJB, italics mine)

If we believe Yeshua's words, that he does not lie and that his word is truth, then this passage should be all we need to make speech ethics a high priority. Some day we will have to give an account of ourselves for all of our trash talk.

So let's spend some time taking a peek at the riches of Jewish discussion about speech ethics. Meet *lashon hora*.

The What of Tasteful Talk: What is *Lashon Hora*?

Lashon hora, literally "evil tongue," therefore, evil speech—is a term used broadly in Jewish life to indicate inappropriate speech in its multiple guises. You would expect the term to apply to "bad-mouthing" someone by telling lies about them, and it does. But it may surprise you to learn that the term is also used more narrowly of a particular kind of forbidden speech, that is, making *true* comments that portray someone in a negative light. For Jewish speech ethics, even telling the truth is often wrong. Let's look at that!

How many times have you heard someone justify the bad things they said about someone else by saying, "Well, it's true!" From Judaism's point of view, this is no defense at all. Bad-mouthing this person still pollutes the relational air. If it's not true, necessary, and kind, it should never be loosed on the world.

And sometimes even positive or innocuous information can be deadly. If you doubt what I am saying, listen to Rabbi Joseph Telushkin as he tells us the story of a hero whose life was ruined because someone else could not keep his mouth shut concerning what they thought was good news about him.

Oliver Sipple, a former Marine, was standing in the right place at the right time in 1975 when Sara Jane Moore aimed a gun at President Gerald Ford. Sipple grabbed her arm, deflecting her aim so that Ford was not injured, thus becoming an instant hero. Reporters flocked to interview him, and he begged them not to write anything about him. But this was a hot story, and they thought he was just being modest. They ignored his request, writing human-interest stories about Sipple, including the fact that he was active in gay causes in the San Franscisco Bay area.

What they did not know was that Sipple had never "come out" to his parents. When they heard about the article, his mother stopped talking to him, and when she died four years later, his father told him not to come to the funeral. Sipple then became depressed. He began drinking heavily, became reclusive, depressed, and morbidly obese. He stopped taking good care of himself. Then he was found dead in his apartment, very much alone, at 47 years of age. We can only guess how things would have turned out otherwise if well-meaning journalists had just paid attention to what he asked of them.[3]

There are many other stories just like these, stories of the famous and the unknown, whose lives were damaged or destroyed by others who preferred not to keep their mouths shut. Those of us who love chattering about others need to step back and reconsider. Judaism would remind us that generally, the less said the better.

Here's another example.

Shortly after Senator John McCain's death, someone sent me an article defaming him in strident tones. The person who sent it was politically motivated. When I told her the article was mean-spirited, she said, "But it's true!" We need to get it through our heads that this is not good enough. How many children, and even adults, have taken their lives because of being bullied by people who would protest that what they had said to them or about them was "true"?

Let's get this clear: "True" is not good enough. Perhaps we should all take to heart the aphorism made popular years ago, that we should only say what was "true, necessary, and kind." Good words.

Lashon Hora: Looking Deeper

Besides the well-meaning but unnecessary truth-telling just mentioned, there are other brands of *lashon hora*. One kind is what we might term TMI, too much information. This is purposeless defamatory information. Consider these examples.

- "Mike is kind of slow" (said of someone whose academic progress compares poorly with some others). What in the world is to be gained from making such a statement?

- "Sharon's letting herself go. She needs to take off weight." Even if true, why bother saying so?

- "Bobby is such a sloppy dresser." Again, what's the point of insulting a person's wardrobe choices?

- "Poor Freddy, I doubt if he will ever get married." This is an unnecessary negative prediction.

- One of the greatest theologians of the twentieth century died a hopeless alcoholic on the streets of Los Angeles. George Eldon Ladd was a hardworking man, raised by a negating and critical father. He fought his way up to the top of theological circles, seeking the credibility and acclaim he had long been denied. When he published a crucial work, *Jesus and the Kingdom*, upon which he pinned his hopes of widespread acceptance, a renowned Bible scholar wrote a scathing and denunciatory review. This crushed Ladd, who would never regain his equilibrium. His life became a study of chaos and decay.[4] His marriage fell apart, and he and his adult son ended up as out-of-control alcoholics on the streets of Pasadena.

All of the foregoing are examples of *lashon hora*, true comments that portray someone negatively. And as you have seen, these kinds of statements, even if uttered with benign intent, can be devastating in their effects. Would you agree that these kinds of statements are laced throughout our daily conversations?

Here's a helpful exercise. Simply make the effort to go one week without saying something negative about anyone and without passively allowing that kind of speech in your presence. You will be amazed, embarrassed, and chastened. We are addicted to this stuff, and what's worse, we generally don't even notice. From the vantage point of biblically-grounded Jewish ethics, this is an ethical and spiritual crisis.

Motzi Shem Ra

In contrast to *lashon hora*, which involves true comments, *motzi shem ra* names making false comments that portray someone negatively. Here are some such statements:

• "I'll bet Marty likes to hang out in the bar because nobody else even pretends to care about him." This is such a global statement, nasty too, and it cannot possibly be validated as true. And since you do not know that your assessment of Marty is true, it is grounded only in your unproven opinion. How about keeping your opinion to yourself?

• "Even though she shows up at some of our events, I'm not sure Rachael really believes as we do." If you are "not sure," then there are insufficient grounds in fact for this statement. Since Jewish ethics require us to give people the benefit of the doubt, this criticism is to be presumed to be false—and thus *motzi shem ra.*

• "There goes Laura. Another Democrat. Democrats don't care about evil." Oh, really? All Democrats? Democrats as a class? Where did you do your research? What kind of evil? This global statement cannot be proven to be true, should be considered false unless proven otherwise, and should not pass your lips.

• "To tell you the truth, I can't figure out why Chris is a Republican. Everybody knows Republicans only care about the rich and balancing the budget." Oh really? Everybody knows? All of them? Republicans as a class? They *only* care about these things? And therefore, Chris too? How do you know these things, great guru in the sky?

Such statements, where the assessment of another is negative but without sufficient basis in fact, are all examples of what Jewish life calls *motzi shem ra.*

Jewish speech ethics goes even deeper, far deeper than we can in this brief chapter. But even without doing so, there is no doubt that all of us will find ourselves nailed in the process by a final category. Consider *rechilut*.

What Is *Rechilut*?

Rechilut refers to statements that sow discord between people or cause people to think badly of others. This is gossip or tale-bearing. It is the norm in our culture, and again, it stinks. But we have become so accustomed to the stench, we do not notice.

The term is derived from the root Torah text upon which all Jewish discussion of speech ethics is based, *Vayikra*/Leviticus 19:16, which says, "Do not go around spreading slander among your people, but also don't stand idly by when your neighbor's life is at stake; I am ADONAI" (CJB). A *rachil* is something of a peddler. He or she picks something up here and unloads it there. The *rachil* just loves going around and spreading the dirt.

The term is used six times in the Older Testament: once in the Torah, twice in Proverbs, twice in Jeremiah, and once in Ezekiel. Looking at these passages gives a feel for its meaning:

• Leviticus 19:16—"Do not go around spreading slander among your people, but also don't stand idly by when your neighbor's life is at stake; I am ADONAI" (CJB).

• Proverbs 11:13—"A gossip goes around revealing secrets, but a trustworthy person keeps a confidence" (CJB).

- Proverbs 20:19—"A gossip goes around revealing secrets, so don't get involved with a talkative person" (CJB).

- Jeremiah 6:28—"All of them are total rebels, spreading slanderous gossip; they are bronze and iron, [inferior metals,] all of them corrupt" (CJB).

- Jeremiah 9:4—"Beware of your friends; do not trust anyone in your clan. For every one of them is a deceiver, and every friend a slanderer" (NIV).

- Ezekiel 22:9—"In you, people gossip (*anshe rachil*—men of gossip; gossipers) to the point of inciting bloodshed; in you are those who go to eat on the mountains; in you, they commit lewd acts" (CJB).

Rechilut—being a *rachil*—therefore refers to people who exalt their own social standing by lowering the status of others through spreading defamatory information about them. A *rachil* is a "put-down artist." He or she peddles gossip in order to feel superior to others or to win social recognition for having such "interesting" information. Here is what this conduct looks like:

- "I hate to tell you this, Sharon, but Debra has been bad-mouthing you behind your back. She is not really your friend." Actually, here the speaker is doing just what she accuses Debra of doing—badmouthing someone behind their back.

- "Meryl, just some friendly advice. Don't trust Sandy so much. I hear she's not to be trusted." This typical report, "I heard XYZ about someone," is a *rechilut* kind of gossip. The speaker's "friendly advice," a highly negative put-down of Sandy, is a subtle plea for cementing her relationship with Meryl. This is as common as dust, but worthless in God's sight.

The most gripping example of *rechilut* is when someone is accused and convicted of a crime on the evidence of lying witnesses. Of such witnesses, the Torah requires the following:

> If a malicious witness comes forward and
> gives false testimony against someone,
> then both the men involved in the con-
> troversy are to stand before ADONAI, be-
> fore the *cohanim* and the judges in office
> at the time. The judges are to investigate
> carefully. If they find that the witness is ly-
> ing and has given false testimony against
> his brother, you are to do to him what he
> intended to do to his brother. In this way,
> you will put an end to such wickedness
> among you. Those who remain will hear
> about it, be afraid and no longer commit
> such wickedness among you. Show no
> pity: life for life, eye for eye, tooth for tooth,
> hand for hand, foot for foot.
> (Deut 19:16–21, CJB)

Most people don't know that this is where we get the "eye for an eye, tooth for a tooth" passage. The passage is not about revenge: it is about judicial justice. This is meant to set a limit on the justice that is exacted: You may only do to a false witness what that witness maliciously intended would happen to the falsely accused. And for the purposes of our investigation of *rechilut*, we should note that making knowingly false accusations earns the equivalent punishment for false witnesses. They deserve to have false defamations circulated about them. An eye for an eye.

Obviously, God takes this most seriously, and so should we. Traditional Judaism sees this passage as applying to witnesses in collusion with the plaintiff, and witnesses who were not even present at the event about which they are testifying.

Believe it or not, we have just touched the fringes of what Jewish thought has to say about unethical speech. There are more terms and more gradations of the subject, along with extensive discussion about extenuating circumstances, when it is permitted to seek and to speak negative information about someone, and the limits placed even on that practice.[5] But so as to not overwhelm us, let's settle for the three terms we have so far considered. To review, we have identified:

Lashon hora—Reporting something true but negative about someone

Motzi shem ra—Reporting something false but negative about someone

Rechilut—Undermining someone's social standing and elevating your own through what you report about a person; gossip and slander

I think we will all agree with the words of the movie *Apollo 13* with regard to the vast reach of these issues: "Houston, we have a problem."

The How: A Recipe for Stamping Out *Lashon Hora*

What should we do about all of this? *Eat This Book!* promotes an apprenticeship not simply of knowing, but of *doing*. Apprentices learn to *do* something by doing it.

So here are some steps we can take to "clean up our act," moving from evil speech to tasteful talk.

1. **Commit to implementing incremental changes in your speech habits.** Read wise books on this subject that are pitched to your interest level and stylistic preferences. You will be greatly helped by heeding the counsel of gifted spiritual teachers like Mark Kinzer in his *Taming the Tongue*, Joseph Telushkin in *Words that Hurt, Words That Heal*, the works of the Chofetz Chaim, and also a recent and detailed book from a religious Jewish perspective, *False Facts and True Rumors: Lashon HaRa in Contemporary Culture* by Daniel Z. Feldman. Reading these books is guaranteed to awaken and sensitize you to the many ways we've learned to tolerate shoddy communications of all kinds, from others and from ourselves. These books will make you

eager to form an inward spiritual alliance with God based on this ancient prayer, "Lᴏʀᴅ, place a guard at my mouth, a sentry at the door of my lips" (Ps 141:3. GNT).

2. **Meditate on core texts.** In reading the Bible and good books about *lashon hora*, you will come across texts that grab you. Why not chew on these throughout the day? You'll find yourself being purified by the process. Here are some examples from Scripture:

• "May the words of my mouth and the thoughts of my heart be acceptable in your presence, Aᴅᴏɴᴀɪ, my Rock and Redeemer" (Ps 19:14, CJB).

• "Set a guard, Aᴅᴏɴᴀɪ, over my mouth; keep watch at the door of my lips" (Ps 141:3, CJB).

• "Out of the same mouth come blessing and cursing! Brothers, it isn't right for things to be this way. A spring doesn't send both fresh and bitter water from the same opening, does it? Can a fig tree yield olives, my brothers? or a grapevine, figs? Neither does salt water produce fresh" (Jas 3:10–12, CJB).

3. **Partner with others.** Making yourself accountable is a great way to form new habits. Find one or more friends you can partner with in this project of cleaning up your act. Perhaps you can all agree to read the same book, either together, *havruta*-style, or individually, and agree to a Zoom or Facetime discussion at set intervals, every week or two, even once a month. I can

guarantee that all of you will have stories to tell about how you were dismayed or confused by something, or about a connection you found that made you more aware of your own violations of ethical speech.

4. **Choose your own area for improvement each week, and keep an accountability diary at the end of each day, monitoring how you did with that practice.**

It will really be a simple thing, but very powerful, for you to intentionally plan what area of improvement you will be pursuing each week, and within that, what you will pursue each day. What kind of careless speech are you looking to uproot? What habits of thoughtful speech are you looking to establish? Incremental change works best, so force yourself to think in small steps.

In that accountability diary at the end of the day, you can reflect on how well you did, what you learned, and make a note on something you need to work on. Celebrate every improvement or insight gained. Judaism uses this approach to character improvement. Broadly, this is an aspect of *Mussar*, the Jewish discipline of character development.[6]

You cannot and will not change everything about your speech habits in one week, one month, or even one year. Old habits die hard, and sometimes awareness takes a long time to come out of hiding. Simply growing in awareness is a huge advance. To foster change, develop a spirit of gradualism.

FOR BETTER DIGESTION

1. Think of someone you know who has never had a bad word to say about anyone else. What do you and others think of this person?

2. Think of someone you know who is just the opposite—always finding fault and spreading negativity. What do you and others think of this person?

3. As you read or watch the news, notice how often even famous people get themselves in trouble by needlessly opening their mouths.

4. From considering these questions, what changes will you commit to making for your own life and reputation?

MORE FOOD FOR THOUGHT

(For complete publication information, please see the For Further Reading section.)

HaRav Yisroel Meir Kagen zt"l, *Sefer Chofetz Chaim—English Translation Arranged for Daily Study*

Accessible translation of materials from the Chofetz Chaim (Israel Meir Kagan), the foundational Jewish authority on ethical speech. Comprehensive, unpretentious, and authoritative.

Daniel Z. Feldman, *False Facts and True Rumors: Lashon HaRa in Contemporary Culture*

Clear, authoritative, brilliant categorization and treatment of the laws of ethical speech as applied to contemporary challenges. Authoritative and practical. No one serious about this subject can afford to miss this volume.

Mark S. Kinzer, *Taming the Tongue*

True to Dr. Kinzer's usual form, well-written and well-organized, a penetrating exhortation about the speech ethics to which our faith requires us to adhere. Everyone should read this book, and every community of faith would benefit from taking it seriously. User-friendly.

Joseph Telushkin, *Words That Hurt, Words That Heal, Revised Edition: How the Words You Choose Shape Your Destiny*

Rabbi Telushkin is a superior writer who in this book shows us the horrific damage *lashon hora* (evil speech) does in modern life. Taken from contemporary sources, his illustrations are a sober indictment of how far our standards of public speech have fallen. Get this book.

TAKE-OUT

Yes, the tongue is a fire, a world of wick-
edness. The tongue is so placed in our
body that it defiles every part of it, setting
ablaze the whole of our life; and it is set on
fire by Gei-Hinnom itself. For people have
tamed and continue to tame all kinds of
animals, birds, reptiles and sea creatures;
but the tongue no one can tame—it is an
unstable and evil thing, full of death-deal-
ing poison! (Ya'akov/James 3:6–8, CJB)

CHAPTER FOUR

INVITING OTHERS TO THE FEAST

Inviting others to the great End-Time God-Feast is a great privilege—and it's so easily bungled. I should know: Bungling is my learning style, and I've learned a lot! Faith-sharing should be and could be one of your deepest satisfactions. It is for me. In this chapter and the next, you will learn how it's done. But first, meet one of my characteristic bungles. It might be one of yours, too.

I bungle when I am so eager to share something that I mangle the relational moment, unprepared to wait, inattentive to the rhythms of interpersonal communication. Instead, I just barge in, blurt out, and get nowhere. Sometimes, the problem is timing. I don't read the moment, I don't bother to discern readiness. I'm just bursting at the seams like a seven-year-old kid who's had way too much chocolate.

Other times, I fail to get relationally aligned. Maybe you have done this, too. About fifty years ago, a few friends and I visited Westwood, the Los Angeles neighborhood surrounding UCLA. We were all eager to share our faith with anyone who would listen. This was in the early 1970s, and we would have been termed Jesus freaks by just about anyone there.

I remember I had this young guy backed up against a wall, and I was bombarding him with the Good News of Yeshua. It was a religious data dump. I was the dumper and he was the dumpee! At that point, a friend who was supervising all of us on this excursion came up behind me, tapped me on the shoulder, said "Excuse me," and moved me aside. Then he asked the dumpee the magical question: "Hi. My name is Moishe. What's your name?"

With shock and embarrassment I realized I had never bothered introducing myself or asking the fellow's name! I had turned what should have been a very personal conversation into a collision with a dump truck. Not good.

Maybe you are bursting to tell someone about your faith. Or maybe you have taken a blood oath never to be caught in that situation. In either case, this chapter is for you. For sure, a lot of people are like me, and sometimes there's a lot of bungling between here and getting things right. But I figure if our message about Yeshua is good news, the experience of sharing Yeshua-faith should be a pleasant one for all concerned. The time has come to move our dump trucks out of the way and find ways to make the Good News sound like what it is: good news, and something others will welcome.

This is the heart of the matter, remembering that faith-sharing is intensely relational. In our task-oriented, bullet-pointed world, this means we need to ramp up how much we value relationships. After all, Yeshua reminded us that the two most pivotal commandments are each relational: The *Sh'ma*, that is, loving God with all our hearts, souls, and minds, and also loving our neighbors as we love ourselves.

And yes, Yeshua compares this kind of community-building to inviting people to a feast. Who doesn't love a feast? But considering the bad reputation Yeshua and his followers have among Jewish people, Jews are most often likely to decline the invitation. To share Yeshua's Good News effectively with our people, we're going to need to acknowledge the wretched reputation of Yeshua's flock—too often wolves in sheep's clothing. We need to make the message of Yeshua good news again.

So let's look together at promising ways to help other Jews see that the message of Yeshua is really good news for Jew and Gentile alike, and not simply somebody else's strange—and threatening—religious fixation.

When the Good News Is Not So Good and What to Do About It

If you were to ask the average American to summarize the message Yeshua's followers are called to proclaim, what kind of answer would you get? How about these?

• It's John 3:16—"For God so loved the world that he gave his only begotten son so that whoever believes in him should not perish but have everlasting life."

• It's the promise that if you believe in Jesus you will be forgiven for your sins and go to heaven instead of hell when you die.

• It's the message that everyone is going to hell except the people who agree with Christians.

Most people are not rushing to grab hold of these messages, certainly not most Jews. But if we will examine what Yeshua's representatives, the apostles, proclaimed to both Jewish and non-Jewish audiences, we will discover their message was more nuanced, and the most positive message imaginable.

Bible scholars call the core message preached by the Apostles "the *kerygma*." The word means "proclamation or preaching" in Greek. Here is a sample of what their *kerygma* was, as Peter, also known as Kepha, summarized it.

> This is the message of Good News for the people of Israel—that there is peace with God through Jesus Christ, who is Lord of all. You know what happened throughout Judea, beginning in Galilee, after John began preaching his message of immersion. And you know that God anointed Yeshua of Nazareth with the Holy Spirit and with

power. Then Yeshua went around doing good and healing all who were oppressed by the devil, for God was with him.

And we apostles are witnesses of all he did throughout Judea and in Jerusalem. They put him to death by hanging him on a cross, but God raised him to life on the third day. Then God allowed him to appear, not to the general public, but to us whom God had chosen in advance to be his witnesses. We were those who ate and drank with him after he rose from the dead. And he ordered us to preach everywhere and to testify that Yeshua is the one appointed by God to be the judge of all—the living and the dead. He is the one all the prophets testified about, saying that everyone who believes in him will have their sins forgiven through his name. (Acts 10:36–43, NLT)

Notice how compact and incisive this is. Peter is not all over the map here but is giving a summation all can understand and either accept or reject.

On an earlier occasion, Peter reminded his hearers about the implications of this message, encompassing the well-being of the entire world, which he terms, "The restoration of all the things that God spoke about long ago through the mouth of His holy prophets" (Acts 3:22, TLV). This is no provincial just-me-and-my-crowd message. Even people who don't accept it would agree that this message, if true, is good news for everyone and everything.

Before signing up as an advocate for this revolution, we will need to get over the hump of an icky subject—judgment—something that gets a lot of bad press.

Judgment: Good News or Bad News?

Let's remember that judgment is not some sort of New Testament Fundamentalist fetish. Whenever Yeshua's representatives talk about judgment, what they say resonates well with the entire Older Testament, where judgment is both good news and bad news. Consider this for example:

> Let the heavens be glad, and let the earth
> rejoice; let the sea roar, and all that fills
> it; let the field exult, and everything in it!
> Then shall all the trees of the forest sing
> for joy before the LORD, for he comes, for
> he comes to judge the earth. He will judge
> the world in righteousness, and the peo-
> ples in his faithfulness.
> (Ps 96:11–13, ESV)

Judgment is actually *good* news! It's something to sing about! It's a message of rescuing humanity and the world from the worst kind of entropy—the drag of evil. This judgment is only bad news for those who have lived to victimize the poor and powerless. But it's the best news for the victimized and those who have walked toward the light and not in darkness. Whenever the subject of judgment comes up when discussing Yeshua-faith, remind people that it's something for good people to celebrate. While no one is perfectly good, it makes no sense to imagine that God is indifferent to the distinction between a generous and caring childcare worker and a mugger searching for his next victim.

Using the prospect of God's judgment as a club to drive people toward Yeshua is a lousy idea. Don't go there. Even the apostles didn't go there!

Talking about the message Yeshua's earliest revolutionaries shared, Neal Rees, former International Coordinator for World Horizons International, forcefully reminds us that "the basic apostolic *kerygma* fails to mention hell as a motive for accepting the gospel message," adding that "the apostles were perfectly capable of evangelizing without threatening their hearers with hell... [and] this is never developed in evangelistic preaching."[1] While this doesn't mean there is no such thing as hell, it does mean that the way we talk about it needs attention.

Much of the fixation on finding heaven, and avoiding hell, may be traced to the missions movement of the 18th and 19th centuries. The hymns of this period are full of such images which motivated hundreds, even thousands of people to spend and lose their lives in dangerous, hostile, foreign cultures. These were heroes and heroines, bringing the message of Yeshua where it had never before been heard. As a measure of this devotion, consider that it used to be customary for missionaries from the China Inland Mission to pack their belongings in coffins as they journeyed off to their mission fields. Why? Because they would need the coffins out there, as they weren't expecting to come back. These giants deserve our profound respect. But their motivational structure need not be our default position. This was not the way the apostles went about their task; it was not the motivation that drove them, and it need not be our approach either.

Getting Beyond Individualism

We have been seeing that the project launched by Yeshua and his earliest followers is the best news there is, pointing toward a renovated cosmos set free from sin, sickness, and death. Because this is so, we need to get out of the habit of thinking of Yeshua as simply anyone's "personal savior." We need a big-picture vision. The Apostle Paul, who was an expert in such things, says this in writing to Timothy, "We have our hope set on a living God who is the deliverer of all humanity, especially of those who trust" (1 Tim 4:10, CJB). Elsewhere, he compares this community to a body, not a collection of individuals, but an interrelated, interdependent whole. Look what Paul says about the redemptive reach of Yeshua's work for us:

> He is head of the Body, the Messianic
> Community—he is the beginning, the
> firstborn from the dead, so that he might
> hold first place in everything. For it
> pleased God to have his full being live in
> his Son and through his Son to reconcile
> to himself all things, whether on earth
> or in heaven, making peace through him,
> through having his Son shed his blood by
> being executed on a stake.
> (Col 1:18–20, CJB)

Instead of being simply a personal savior, the Messiah is intended to be redeemed humanity's common denominator. As such, he is the Savior of entire classes of humanity, the Redeemer of the cosmos itself, not just of little bitty me, or even big strong you! Sharing the Good News is not picking off stragglers. It is something more. Paul helps us again, relaying what God had shown him:

> He has made known to us his secret plan,
> which by his own will he designed be-
> forehand in connection with the Messiah

and will put into effect when the time
is ripe—*his plan to place everything in
heaven and on earth under the Messiah's
headship.*
(Eph 1:9–10, CJB, italics mine)

"Everything in heaven and on earth!" That's pretty big, don't you think?

Of course, there *is* a personal dimension to all this! As the Divine Presence awakens our inner selves so that the status of our relationship with God comes together in our minds, we will of course realize that Yeshua deserves our thanks, our obedience, and our honor. As we walk in this path, the essential Being of God, the Divine Presence, bonds with our essential selves (our spirits), and works within us conforming us to the image of Yeshua—reshaping us to increasingly resemble the Man from Galilee, who always honored his Father.

This is what Paul refers to when he says that "those whom he (God) knew in advance, he also determined in advance would be conformed to the pattern of his Son, so that he might be the firstborn among many brothers" (Ro 8:29, CJB).

By now all of us can see that the message about Yeshua is truly good news. But how might we package what we have to say about Yeshua so it comes across as good news about the world and our curious friends?

Let's look at ways our friends might discover Yeshua's Good News as good news for themselves.

Four Encounters

Charles Kraft was one of my mentors when I was in graduate school. He taught us to think of three bridges people cross in coming to Yeshua faith. He calls these the truth encounter, the power encounter, and the allegiance encounter.

In a *truth encounter*, people embrace the truth-claims of the Bible and its message, adopting Scripture's worldview and perspective as a standard against which other truth claims are to be measured. To our modern eyes and ears this seems bigoted or at least restrictive. But this is not some quirky fundamentalist artifact. Really, this is how it has always been, and the true and living God has always been clear-cut about this.

Throughout our Scriptures, the God of Israel makes and justifies exclusivist claims. The Bible and our tradition report how he was vexed because our ancestors thought they could worship him and idols as well. God says clearly, "That won't do."

> You are to fear ADONAI your God, serve him
> and swear by his name. You are not to fol-
> low other gods, chosen from the gods of
> the peoples around you.
> (Deut 6:13–14, CJB)

> You are to love *ADONAI* your God with all
> your heart, all your being and all your re-
> sources.
> (Deut 6:5, CJB)

> I am *ADONAI* your God, who brought you
> out of the land of Egypt, out of the abode
> of slavery. You are to have no other gods
> before me. (Ex 20:2–3, CJB)

Although all truth is God's truth, and although truth is truth wherever it is found, spiritual truth needs to measure up to what our Scriptures say, that is, if you want something dependable. Isaiah the Prophet said it this way: "To the law and to the testimony! If they do not speak according to this word, it is because they have no dawn" (Isa 8:20, NASB 1995). So, in a *truth encounter*, people embrace the truth claims of the Bible and its message, adopting Scripture's worldview and perspective as a standard against which other spiritual truth claims are to be measured.

I knew an electrical engineer who first picked up the Bible to discount its claims, and especially its claims of Yeshua. He told me that as he read Scripture, eventually, while he still had questions, he became convinced that the Bible would somewhere reliably address his concerns. He had had a truth encounter. It didn't come from a weak mind, but a pliable spirit.

In a *power encounter* we submit to the power and claims of the *Ruach HaKodesh*, the Holy Spirit, and renounce all other sources of spiritual empowerment in submission to the Divine Presence. I've got lots of stories to bring this home to you. When I was leading a synagogue of Jewish Yeshua-believers in Beverly Hills, a woman and her husband began attending. She was actually an Arab from Algeria who had come to faith in Yeshua, whereupon God told her to come and worship with Jews. (Yes, she was startled!) So, she came with her American husband. Both of them had been practicing Sokko Gakkai Buddhism, complete with a Buddhist altar in their home, where they chanted every day. She had given it all up, but her husband, whom we will call Bill, was not convinced. I asked him if I could pray with him that the true and living God might show him that this was something he needed to part with. He said, "Sure." And so I prayed for him. It took about thirty seconds. No big deal. But then again, we need to remember who it is to whom I prayed!

A few days later I got a report from Bill. And this next part you may not believe, but here goes: A large ball of fire, a kind of spiritual fire, manifested in their apartment, yes, scaring the chants off of them! Bill was convinced. What happened was a collision of the powers, a power encounter in which the God of Israel demonstrated his supremacy over other claimants for our spiritual allegiance.

Another story: Fifty years ago I met a young woman who had been deeply into astrology when she came to Yeshua faith. She wanted to throw her astrology books away as a sign of her breaking with that form of spiritual empowerment. But she found she just couldn't bring herself to do it. She was encountering some sort of resistance. It was as if these books held some sort of power over her, and she needed help to break it. She called some people from our group to come pray with her and help her get rid of the books. And she did.

This is not the way we usually talk. I can't blame you if you think all of this sounds superstitious. But for now, let me urge you to suspend judgment. People formerly immersed in other spiritual paths often encounter some sort of spiritual turmoil when opting for Yeshua-faith. This is what we term a power encounter. But the choice must be made, and it makes all the difference.

The *allegiance encounter* is closely related. Here we take a stand pledging allegiance to Israel's God through His Messiah. Even though modern pluralistic and often autonomous humanity finds this strange, vowing allegiance is the native tongue of the Bible. Consider the *Sh'ma* and its reminder,, "Listen, O Israel! The LORD is our God, the LORD alone. And you must love the LORD your God with all your heart, all your soul, and all your strength" (Dt 6:4–5, NLT).

We Jews who embrace Yeshua as Messiah know that just as Israel in the past needed to show their respect for God by showing proper honor to his Prophets, so we show proper honor to God by honoring Yeshua, his Messiah. Paul drives this home when he writes this to the Philippians:

> God raised him to the highest place and
> gave him the name above every name;
> that in honor of the name given Yeshua,
> every knee will bow—in heaven, on earth
> and under the earth—and every tongue
> will acknowledge that Yeshua the Messiah
> is ADONAI—to the glory of God the Father.
> (Phil 2:9-11, CJB)

Here we are not talking merely about beliefs but about our will and our choices. In pledging allegiance to God, we promise to be loyal to him in the details of life. To better understand how this works out on the ground in a Jewish context, let's add a fourth encounter, the *covenantal encounter*.

Dr. Kraft is a product of his culture and so I cannot blame him for leaving something out that is intrinsic to the Jewish historical experience—the covenantal encounter. It requires that we come to terms with our identity and responsibilities as part of a people who have a history with God expressed in mutually binding agreements. We call these covenants. You might define a covenant as "a structured agreement pledging faithfulness and defining responsibilities." Through them, we pledge our faithfulness to *HaShem* and he pledges his faithfulness to us. Because we are all heirs to our ancestors' covenants with our God, they have continued implications for us now.

This kind of covenantal understanding may seem weird because there's a wide cultural distance between secularized modern life and the worldview of biblical times and cultures. We default to autonomy and individualism, but these covenants grow out of a collectivist mentality, where identity is grounded not simply in *who* you are but in *whose* you are. The big question is this: "Of what larger group am I a part?"

The Bible presents Israel as a people chosen for the sake of others. And to pull that off, God created and redeemed this entire people for himself. He calls us "the people whom I formed for myself that they might declare my praise" (Isa 43:21, ESV). And elsewhere we are told, "And who is like your people Israel, the one nation on earth whom God went to redeem to be his people, making himself a name and doing for them great and awesome things by driving out before your people, whom you redeemed for yourself from Egypt, a nation and its gods?" (2 Sa 7:23, ESV). This is a people collectively drawn by God to himself into a relationship of mutual faithfulness.

So, when we read and interpret the Bible, and as we consider the choices we make in life, let's remember whose we are, each of us part of a particular people, the offspring of Abraham, Isaac, and Jacob, Sarah, Rebekah, Rachel and Leah, with whom God made structured agreements pledging and requiring faithfulness while defining responsibilities. So let's remember to consider what it means for us to be faithful to him as Jews. Remember, it's not just a personal issue. The question is, "What does it mean for me to honor Yeshua as a faithful Jew?"

We've talked a bit about the content of the invitation-message we have to share with others. It's time now to talk about how to deliver that invitation effectively so that both the messenger and recipient enjoy the process.

If you're saying, "This should be interesting," you're right. Let's go to the next chapter together.

FOR BETTER DIGESTION

1. Have you witnessed or experienced clumsy or even offensive attempts at sharing the Good News of Yeshua? And have you witnessed or experienced effective attempts at doing so? What made the difference?

2. Do you agree or disagree with this statement, and why? "The Good News of Yeshua is essentially about who he is and what he has done for us, and not primarily about what we have to do to 'get saved.'"

3. Do you think we have to tell people the bad news about hell in order to highlight the Good News of Yeshua?

4. Some people believe that the prospect of gaining or losing eternal rewards is essential if we are to believe

in the wisdom of living a virtuous life and the final defeat of evil. Do you agree or disagree, and why?

5. Of the four encounters named in this chapter, how many can you recognize in your own experience?

MORE FOOD FOR THOUGHT

Matthew W. Bates, *Salvation by Allegiance Alone: Rethinking Faith, Works, and the Gospel of Jesus the King*

Following up on insights from Scot McKnight, Bates rightly argues that the faith which the good news of Yeshua demands of us is best understood as allegiance, expressed in obedient living. This is so very true and aligns Yeshua-faith with the call of the *Sh'ma* to love the LORD our God with all our hearts, souls, and minds, a call to allegiance and obedience. While this is not a book for beginners, it is a book for anyone who wants to rightly understand the story of Yeshua and its implications for us all.

Stuart Dauermann, "Six Encounters: Axes of Spiritual Transformation" https://www.interfaithfulness.org/six-encounters-axes-of-spiritual-transformation/

In this blog post, I summarize Kraft's three encounters, add one that I covered in this chapter (the covenantal encounter), plus two more. I think you will find this creative and helpful.

Charles H. Kraft, "What Kind of Encounters Do We Need in Our Christian Witness"? https://missionexus. org/what-kind-of-encounters-do-we-need-in-our-christian-witness/

This is one of many articles to be found by Kraft and others on his construct of the power encounter, allegiance encounter, and truth encounter and their impact on faith-sharing. The online discussion on these matters is interesting, contentious, and well worth exploring. I studied with Dr. Kraft. He is brilliant, and his writing is first-class, even if he is sometimes more imaginative and experimental than I favor.

Scot McKnight, *The King Jesus Gospel: The Original Good News Revisited*

Well written and well argued, this book challenges all to recognize how popular Yeshua-believing culture has turned the gospel into a message of personal salvation, while the apostolic gospel was centered in who Yeshua is, what he did, and the consequences for the cosmos. It is not a message about me and my salvation, but about Him and his enthronement. My only regret about the book is that McKnight sees Jesus as King of the nations, instead of as King of Israel and (therefore) the Savior of the world (see John 4). Readable. Usable. Valuable.

TAKE-OUT

People normally enjoy receiving good news. But the good news of Yeshua is not normally received as good news among Jewish people. Let's do what we can to avoid putting a stumbling block in the way of our people. Let's find ways to present the Good News as something that everyone, including our Jewish friends, would want to celebrate.

CHAPTER FIVE

YESHUA'S GOOD NEWS: A WELL-PRESENTED MEAL

Chefs and restaurateurs take pride not only in the food they serve, but in how it is presented: how it looks on the plate, how pleasing the meal is to the eye even before it passes the palate test. These professionals will be quick to remind us that how the meal is presented is just as important as the meal itself.

The same is true of serving Yeshua's good news to our friends. The message may be true food for the soul, but it won't be appetizing or enjoyable until and unless we pay attention to how it is presented.

That's what we are looking at in this chapter.

Let's begin then with this principle of good news presentation: ***People will only care about your explanations when they covet your experiences.*** **Sharing your experiences with God is like an appetizer for the meal of the good news. We need to first serve our friends a slice of life with God.** This means sharing one or more stories from our own life which will cause our friend to think, "Maybe you have encountered God in a way that I haven't!" Each of these stories is a slice of life with God.

Tell Me a Story

We are talking about storytelling. Advertisers tell stories. Movies tell stories. The Bible is stuffed with stories. It is the universal ancient way of talking about what's important. And we need to get with the program.

While advertisers tell stories to make a sale and get the client to "Yes," our goal is to get our friend to "Maybe." If we've got "Yes" on our mind, we're likely to become manipulative and insistent, and in matters of the Spirit, that's a deal-breaker. It's far better to work toward getting this person to think, "Just maybe my friend has experienced God in a way I want to investigate further." Get them hungry. Get them thirsty for what you have. Be appetizing! Get them to "maybe." And in the back of your mind remember this: No one ever got to "Yes" unless they first got to "Maybe."

It just won't do to tell them any old story, a story about your friend, or that you heard somewhere. It's crucial to tell one that highlights one of your personal experiences with God. And it's easy to find the right words to believably convey a personal story. Such stories automatically bring with them the freight of credibility because people sense they come from the heart. *Again, remember that people will only care about your explanations when they covet your experiences.* So share with them a slice of your life with God.

You will want to tell a story that penetrates the mind and captures the imagination. Here are seven keys to powerful story-telling.

Seven Keys to Telling a Good Story

The first key is: **Assess whom you are talking to.** Who are they? What makes them tick? What turns them on and what turns them off? Where are they at, and what do they seem to be ripe for at this time in their life? Your first focus should be on tuning in to who they are and what matters to them. Then find a story in your life that, as closely as possible, touches on those issues. Always relate what matters to you in a manner that connects with what matters to them.

Sharing your faith-life must never be about making a canned pitch. If you are always telling your story the same way, something is wrong. You are failing to tune in to your particular audience. There is no such thing as a good story. There are only stories that are good for a particular audience at a particular time. So, assess who you are talking to and tailor your presentation to them.

The second key is: **Passion.** Tell a story that matters to you. The only kind of story that will move your friends is one that moves you. Gerry Spence is famous as a remarkably successful personal injury attorney. He attributes much of his success in persuading juries through his passionate storytelling, which he calls speaking from the heart zone:

> Why is the story argument so powerful? It is powerful because it speaks in the language form of the species. Its structure is natural. It permits the storyteller to speak easily, openly, powerfully from the heart zone. It provokes interest. It is an antidote to the worst poison that can be injected into any argument—the doldrums. We are moved by story. A story touches us in our *tenders*, in those soft, unprotected places where our decisions are always made.[1]

Being interesting comes easy once you are excited about something. So, choose a story that matters to you, because only stories that matter to you will matter to others. Heart zone speaks to heart zone. Trying to move people through a story that does not really matter to you will end up feeling phony—phony to you and phony to your friend. It is like a sales pitch. Reject that.

The third key is: **Make sure you are a relatable protagonist.** In a story, as in a movie, the protagonist is the person who leads us through the story and allows us to see it through his or her eyes. The protagonist is the person with whom we identify. When you are sharing your faith journey with someone, you are the protagonist, because it is your story. But you must be a protagonist your listener can relate to. This means you can't present your experience as weird and unrelatable: "I came to believe in Yeshua, and for four days straight, I had visions of heaven!" How nice for you. But you just lost your conversation partner. "Before I believed in Yeshua I was a convicted sex offender!" By this time the other person is dialing 911. Make yourself relatable! Tell your story in a manner such that your friend will say, "I can relate! That could be me!"

The fourth key that makes for a compelling, engrossing story is: **Make sure you have a well-defined antagonist.** The antagonist is the obstacle or negative situation within which you experienced God's intervention. Make your listener feel the weight of the challenge you were facing. The more they feel your pain in this antagonistic situation, the more they will experience the release of the rescue. Make them care about the problem so they will feel relief when it is solved.

The fifth key is: **Identify a turning point.** The stories that engage us have a turning point when things changed for the better. In your case, perhaps it was when you had a breakthrough insight, a time when life shifted for you in some way—a pivot point between before and after. What was it? Can you describe it in a way that makes this come alive for your listener?

The sixth key is: **Portray the right hero.** The hero of the story is not you advertising yourself as gloriously transformed. In the slice-of-life with God approach to faith-sharing, the hero is always the same: It is God.

How did God show up in your situation, how did who God is and what He does begin to make a difference in your life and situation? And how was your encounter with the Jewish Jesus a catalyst in the process?

The seventh and final key is: **Give people a taste of transformation.** How is life different now, if at all, because of the pivotal encounter you chronicle in your story? Don't overstate it, but on the other hand if there is no taste of transformation, your listener will have no occasion to hunger for what you have. *Remember, people will only care about your explanations when they covet your experiences.* But always, be honest: There is more credibility in hesitancy than hype.

Some Final Words About Telling Your Story

In our Western culture, "It's only a story" means that what we are saying is not to be taken too seriously. But this is not the way it is in most of the world and in the Bible. In most of the world and in the Bible itself, storytelling, not lecturing, is the preferred method for conveying spiritual truth, exploring meaning, and motivating action. And in the *Harvard Business Review*, communications guru Carmine Gallo, speaking in the context of sales, tells us why this is true:

> According to molecular biologist John Medina of the University of Washington School of Medicine, the human brain

craves meaning before details. When a listener doesn't understand the overarching idea being presented in a pitch, they have a hard time digesting the information.[2]

The way your listeners will understand the overarching idea—life transformation through encounter with the living God—is through your slice of life with God.

Never allow yourself to feel pressured to "close the deal," and don't try to tell your friend everything you know in this one conversation. The cliché is true: Less is more. What you most want is to nurture in your friend both interest and trust, so they will feel comfortable and even eager to hear more from you another time. Leave room for that, for another time. Give them an appetizer; don't gorge them.

Having interested your friend through sharing a slice of life with God, it may be during this conversation, and it should be in subsequent conversations as well, that you will touch upon one or more of the four encounters we discussed in our prior chapter. Use personal storytelling to explain and illustrate these things. Show your friends that you are eager to hear their stories, too. Leave lots of room for that!

Now let's turn to another appetizing way to present the good news meal.

The Interrogative Style—
The Columbo Method

I have a relative who questions restaurant waiters about the food to be served. Is it gluten-free? What kind of lettuce do they have in the salad? You name it. And as we serve the meal of the good news, we too will be asked questions, a dreaded process for some of us. None of us feel qualified to answer every question we might be asked. And few of us relish being asked hostile questions. In all of this, we need to remember that we who serve the good news meal to others are not so much "answer people" as "question people." We help to guide people through the questions we ask, even more than through the answer we give.

This brings us to the justly famous Lieutenant Columbo.

For those who don't know him, *Columbo* was a TV series about a wily detective of the same name who spent every episode asking questions. Lots of them. Sometimes I would catch myself wondering what it would be like to approach faith-sharing like Columbo did while interrogating suspects. I was therefore delighted to run across Gregory Koukl's *Tactics: A Game Plan for Discussing Your Christian Convictions.*[3] He takes up about half of this book applying Columbo's questioning strategies to faith-sharing. Here's my summary of his main points.

Columbo tried to get people to confess their crimes. He did this by asking brilliantly incisive questions. We try to get people to confess the weakness of their objections, and eventually to confess that Yeshua truly is the One of whom Moses and the Prophets wrote. We can do this like Columbo did, by asking questions ourselves. It is creative and fun. But how?

First, when we advocate for Yeshua we need to remain polite and deferential. You will find this is always true of Columbo. He is always interrogating murder suspects, but he always calls them Mr., Mrs., or Miss So-and-So, or Sir or Ma'am. His tone of voice, his comments, everything about him is polite. He comes across as a bumbling, ostensibly harmless inquirer who is just trying to tie down some loose ends by asking a few questions.

This reminds us that when we are seeking to share our faith with others, we should always be low-key. We have nothing to gain and everything to lose by putting people on the defensive. Let's avoid that! Instead, let's always work at paying meticulous attention to how they answer our questions. Being aggressive will always cause people to shut down. But being polite and inquisitive will help our friends remain open and self-disclosing. And we should spend most of our time listening.

We especially need to avoid, "I'm right and you're wrong and I'm going to show you why." Sadly, it is the default approach of very many people. It is not only worthless—it alienates people. Falling into that trap will leave us talking to ourselves! So be inquisitive, attentive, and polite.

A polite and inquisitive approach also honors the other person because we are being curious about what they think and attentive to their answers. This builds trust and a climate of self-disclosure.

This inquisitive approach is a harmless and non-intrusive manner for learning what our friend believes and does not believe, and why. Since we want to persuade people about Yeshua, it pays for us to know as much as possible about their convictions, arguments, and pet peeves. The better we know our audience, the better we will communicate with them.

People with objections about Yeshua faith will often undermine their own confidence when they try to articulate and defend their views. This may be the first time they have ever sought to fully articulate what their position is, and often, in the process, they talk themselves out of their objections.

Being an attentive inquirer protects us from being in the hot seat and on the defensive. We are not making a statement and not taking and defending a position. When you make statements, you can be accused of being wrong. But when you ask questions, the worst that can happen is that you come across as uninformed. That's a big difference. Besides, in any discussion, the burden of proof lies with the person making the truth claims. And in this case, if the other person is articulating or attacking a position, they will be the ones who need to prove their point!

How the Columbo Method Happens on the Ground

You get the opportunity to be Lieutenant Columbo when someone makes a statement differing with or dismissing faith in God, biblical faith, or Yeshua-faith. Here are some examples:

"All religions are the same."

"Religion is a kind of infantile make-believe. I don't see how anyone intelligent can go there."

"Jesus never claimed to be anything but a rabbi, a Jewish teacher. It is people like Paul who went and made a god out of him, probably to merchandise him to the Gentile world."

"The Bible is a bunch of superstitious drivel written by prescientific people."

Sometimes, it's clothes that make a statement. Koukl tells about a young woman at a checkout counter who wore a pentagram around her neck. Koukl picked up on the significance of it, and in response to his question, the woman said she was a pagan. Maybe you will instead encounter someone wearing an anti-religious T-shirt or displaying a bumper sticker with some sort of anti-religious statement. It's not a good idea to do battle with such a person. The Columbo Method gives us a better way to engage. The trick is to ask gentle but penetrating questions.

Koukl helps us out by suggesting three kinds of questions Columbo models for us. We can see these as three phases of our conversation.

The Columbo Method: The Three Questions

The first question is the *What Question,* where we ask our friend about what she (or he) meant by the objection they raised. We would phrase our question like this: "What do you mean by that?" or, "Could you help me to understand you better? What did you mean by what you just said?" You get the drift. This kind of clarifying question may be repeated as needed to drill down into what your friend means by what he or she is saying or wearing. And there is nothing argumentative about it. Just remember to be deferential and low-key.

Let's apply the What Question to each of the sample statements we just considered.

"All religions are the same."

In what ways do you see them as the same?

"Religion is a kind of infantile make-believe. I don't see how anyone intelligent can go there."

What makes you choose the word "infantile"? I'm curious to know more.

"Jesus never claimed to be anything but a rabbi, a Jewish teacher. It is people like Paul who went and made a god out of him, probably to merchandise him to the Gentile world."

Let me understand what you mean. Are you saying that the only kind of statements he made were the kind of statements any Jewish teacher of his time might have made?

"The Bible is a bunch of superstitious drivel written by prescientific people."

Do you mean this about the whole Bible? Could you describe any parts of the Bible that appear superstitious to you?

The second Columbo question is the *Why Question.* Here, gently and without setting off any alarm bells, we ask our inquirer to defend what he or she is saying. For example, "Why do you say that?" or, "Can you tell me how you came to that conclusion?"

Here we are giving our friend the benefit of the doubt by assuming that they have some reason and defense for the position they have just taken. By listening to his or her answer to this question, we stand to discover how this person thinks, we learn something about their experiences, and something about the depth of their convictions and their evidence for them. This is all extremely valuable information. And remember to always behave with utmost courtesy, and to pay conspicuous attention to how your friend responds.

Again, considering our four test statements, the Why Question works this way:

"All religions are the same."

Why do you feel that way? What have you discovered in other religions?

"Religion is a kind of infantile make-believe. I don't see how anyone intelligent can go there."

Why do you think some intelligent people are seriously religious anyway?

"Jesus never claimed to be anything but a rabbi, a Jewish teacher. It is people like Paul who went and made a god out of him, probably to merchandise him to the Gentile world."

Why do you think Yeshua's claims to be the Messiah are no different from any rabbi's claims? Why do you think Paul wanted to merchandise him to the Gentile world?

"The Bible is a bunch of superstitious drivel written by prescientific people."

Why do you think that prescientific people would necessarily produce superstitious drivel? What do you make of people like Socrates, Aristotle, and Plato who helped to form the backbone of modern logic and persuasion?

This brings us to the third Columbo question: the *"Have You Ever Considered This?" Question.* We ask this kind of question after it seems that the What and Why questions have been exhausted. Here we gently seek to plant doubt in the mind of our friend about his or her own position. By doing so, we open them to considering the sturdier ground and better answers we are advocating.

Koukl says this is the phase of the dialogue where we place a stone in their shoe—some question, perspective, or issue that will challenge them in some way, an issue they will have to deal with down the road. This will be very effective if we have first done the groundwork of listening to their answers to well-conceived What and Why questions. The more adept we are at understanding others' positions, the deeper we can go in this step of the Columbo Method. And we can constantly improve our capacity to interact with such people incisively, sensitively, and respectfully.

Let's apply this third question to the statements we have been examining together:

"All religions are the same."

Have you ever considered how difficult it is to reconcile that Buddhism, (which does not speak of a personal God) and Islam (which speaks of a God who is a high and lofty monarch but in no sense a parent) can be the same God as found in Judaism or Christianity (which speak of God as Father, and us as his children)?

"Religion is a kind of infantile make-believe. I don't see how anyone intelligent can go there."

Have you ever considered how to reconcile this with the fact that some of the greatest scientific minds of this and past generations have been deeply religious people? For example, have you investigated the religious convictions of Blaise Pascal, one of the greatest geniuses in the field of mathematical theory and the physical sciences, or the convictions of Sir Isaac Newton and more recently geneticist Francis Collins, the Director of the Human Genome Project and now the Director of the National Institutes of Health? What do you think causes a promi-

nent scientist to be religious? Is it rational to say these people are not intelligent? Is it possible you are excluding such data because of your presuppositions?

"Jesus never claimed to be anything but a rabbi, a Jewish teacher. It is people like Paul who went and made a god out of him, probably to merchandise him to the Gentile world."

Have you ever considered that in the only firsthand records we have of what Yeshua said about himself, the Gospels, he makes statements that no mere rabbi could make in good conscience? And if Paul admitted that his message about Yeshua, the resurrected Jewish Messiah, is "foolishness to the Greeks," why would he even try to present this message to them if it were not true?

"The Bible is a bunch of superstitious drivel written by prescientific people."

Have you ever considered that the great genius Isaiah Berlin wrote an essay, "The Myth of Progress," in which he addressed our assumption that our culture is categorically superior to what came before, but that's not necessarily true. You must remember these so-called "prescientific people" gave us al-gebra, astronomy, geometry, and all the wealth of Greco-Roman civilization. And of course, the Bible itself has been the rock of Western civilization for thousands of years. These were not grunting cavemen.

A Fourth Columbo Question

To these three Columbo Questions identified by Greg Koukl, I would add one more, also employed by Lieutenant Columbo. It is what we might call the *"Just One More Thing" Question*, which we might also term "the Zinger." Columbo was justly famous for this one. Traditionally it was when he was on the way out the door from one of his sessions of asking "harmless" questions of some suspect. The Zinger was the question most calculated to haunt the person after he left him or her alone, the most penetrating question of all. It's another way of putting a stone in their shoe. The way Columbo asked it was always seemingly innocent, absentminded, and never nasty. But this was where he not only put a stone in their shoes; he also put a knot in their stomachs.

We want to leave our friends captivated by a question they will feel compelled to deal with. Just as we should be prayerful throughout the process of asking the prior three questions, we should be prayerful about identifying just the right Zinger to leave with our friend.

For our four sample areas, our Zinger might be as follows:

"All religions are the same."

Yeshua consistently made statements about himself that stressed his uniqueness, as when he said, "I am the way, the truth, and the life: No one comes to the Father but by me." Author and scholar C. S. Lewis said that a person who says something like this is either a liar, a lunatic, or Lord. Do you see his point? And where do you land on this question?

"Religion is a kind of infantile make-believe. I don't see how anyone intelligent can go there."

Well, if Blaise Pascal, Sir Isaac Newton, and Francis Collins are all giants, then we can't exactly describe them as infants. Would you consider examining their conclusions with me sometime, as two intelligent people having an interesting discussion?

"Jesus never claimed to be anything but a rabbi, a Jewish teacher. It is people like Paul who went and made a god out of him, probably to merchandise him to the Gentile world."

Paul is known as one of the most intelligent and impactful people of the ancient world. Yet he persistently went to the Gentiles in that world with a message they considered foolish, that God had come as a man and been butchered on a Roman cross before being raised from the dead. Why do you think the very savvy Paul persisted in delivering such a message when he knew it came across as stupid to his audience?

"The Bible is a bunch of superstitious drivel written by prescientific people."

If you have never read the Bible from cover to cover, do you think you're entitled to label it as superstitious drivel?

A Final Word About the Columbo Method

You can see that even though we have described four kinds of questions to use in provoking people to consider the claims of Yeshua, this is no wooden formula. It demands creativity and awareness. Part of the fun of this approach is that we keep getting better at it as we learn from experience. In faith-sharing, there is no "magic bullet," and canned, prepackaged presentations are a waste of time. While the Columbo Method is not foolproof, it is extremely effective and valuable. Like wine, it gets better with age, and each conversation is different because each person is different.

I promise you that as you continue to employ this approach to faith-sharing, you are sure to improve your act. And all along the process, you will find that this respectful and insightful approach is just plain fun.

FOR BETTER DIGESTION

1. Can you think of one or more incidents in your life which you could characterize as "a slice of life with God?" If so, then why not go back over the seven characteristics of good storytelling as listed in this chapter, and apply these to how you might relate that incident to a curious friend?

2. What are some objections you have had to religious life or to Yeshua-faith? For those which you have resolved, how did that resolution happen?

3. If you can, identify one or more friends who, while skeptical of religious faith, might be good candidates for you to employ the steps in the Columbo method. Make these people a matter for prayer, and seek out opportunities to engage with them on these matters.

MORE FOOD FOR THOUGHT

Michael L. Brown, *Answering Jewish Objections to Jesus (Five Volumes)*

An extraordinary body of work dealing with a very wide range of Jewish objections to the Messiahship of Yeshua. The books are fascinating, easy to read, and certainly brilliant. Those seeking an orientation to answering the kinds of objections Jewish people are apt to raise about Yeshua-faith will not be disappointed with Brown's superb work.

Gregory Koukl, *Tactics, 10th Anniversary Edition: A Game Plan for Discussing Your Christian Convictions*

Smart, engaging, and immediately practicable. Koukl lays out the Columbo Method (which he calls a tactic) and explains it like no one else could. A fun book which will take the terror out of faith-sharing. User-friendly.

Michael Rydelnik and Edward Blum, *The Moody Handbook of Messianic Prophecy: Studies and Expositions of the Messiah in the Old Testament*

A scholarly treatment of all of the Messianic prophecies you can identify, and many you would not. A monumental work. Even where you might take exception, you will admire the quality of the scholarship here.

A little more difficult to process than Brown's work, but worth the effort.

Annette Simmons, *Whoever Tells the Best Story Wins: How to Use Your Own Stories to Communicate with Power and Impact*

A user-friendly, helpful book on the power of story-telling and how to do it well.

TAKE-OUT

Everything changes when we realize that faith-sharing is more about asking the right questions than it is about claiming to have all the answers.

CHAPTER SIX

ROOM AT THE TABLE: GOD'S SURPRISING GUEST LIST

We've seen how spiritual practices are like meals that sustain our health as we journey toward the Great God-Feast at the end of time.

Yeshua tells us that Jews will be foundational members of the family of God gathered at the A-list banquet table at this Feast. Even so, some of our people will be absent. But why? It's so counterintuitive that this should happen! Yeshua agrees, and tells parables to lament that some who should be at the Feast will fail to return their RSVP.

Here, for example, is one of those parables.

> Once a man gave a banquet and invited
> many people. When the time came for
> the banquet, he sent his slave to tell those
> who had been invited, "Come! Everything
> is ready!" But they responded with a
> chorus of excuses. The first said to him,
> "I've just bought a field, and I have to go

out and see it. Please accept my apologies."
Another said, "I've just bought five yoke of
oxen, and I'm on my way to test them out.
Please accept my apologies." Still another
said, "I have just gotten married, so I can't
come." The slave came and reported these
things to his master. Then the owner of the
house, in a rage, told his slave, "Quick, go
out into the streets and alleys of the city;
and bring in the poor, the disfigured, the
blind and the crippled!" The slave said,
"Sir, what you ordered has been done, and
there is still room." The master said to the
slave, "Go out to the country roads and
boundary walls, and insistently persuade
people to come in, so that my house
will be full. I tell you, not one of those
who were invited will get a taste of my
banquet!"
(Luke 14:16–24, CJB)

Two things are clear here. First, the Master of the
Feast wants a full house. There is nothing stingy about
him; he does everything possible to make sure there
are no empty seats. Second, the problem is not with
him, but with people ignoring the invitation.

Yeshua highlights how needless this is by talking
about early invitees copping out with pathetic excuses.
Even today there will be some people who will miss big

opportunities with God because they don't value the invitation and instead offer excuses.

This is not a new problem, you know. Isaiah, the great Jewish prophet, speaking for ADONAI, talks about it:

> Hear, heaven! Listen, earth! For ADONAI is
> speaking. "I raised and brought up chil-
> dren, but they rebelled against me. An ox
> knows its owner and a donkey its master's
> stall, but Isra'el does not know, my people
> do not reflect. "Oh, sinful nation, a people
> weighed down by iniquity, descendants
> of evildoers, immoral children! They have
> abandoned ADONAI, spurned the Holy One
> of Isra'el, turned their backs on him!"
> (Is 1:2–4, CJB)

Here, Judah meets God's offer of relationship and engagement with contempt. This dynamic appears all over the Bible, showing that even members of God's chosen people have a talent for missing opportunities. Jewish Oral Law picks up on this tension between cho-senness and exclusion when it states, "All Israel have a share in the world to come." This is followed by a qualifying statement, "the following (from within Israel) do not have a share in the world to come," listing categories of those within Israel whose conduct will disqualify them

(TB, Sanhedrin 10:1). In the midst of chosenness—exclusion; in the midst of opportunity—loss.

Nevertheless, no one should contest that the Jewish people have a certain priority in the plans and purposes of God.[1] As the chosen people of God, the Jews are on God's A-List, but not everyone will go. Some will miss out.

Paul talks about the issue of Jewish priority in his Letter to the Romans, employing an allegory about an olive tree. Philip Esler comments:

> [Paul has an] unshakeable belief that Israel had prior place in God's affections and would one day be restored to its privileges. Provoked by non-Israelite arrogance towards Israel among the Roman Christ movement (Rom. 11:13,18,20), Paul constructs an image conveying the insight that the undoubted and vital fact that Israelites and non-Israelites form one social category in Christ in no way means that the differences between these subgroups had been erased. Nor that one is not superior to the other![2]

In contrast to the pretensions of later Christendom, Paul is convinced that, for reasons of God's own choice, the Jewish people remain an especially privileged people. This theme is found throughout the Bible. But we should remember this is always held in tension with the responsibilities that chosenness brings. The Prophet Amos said it best when he reported ADONAI's verdict to Israel, "Of all the families on earth, only you have I intimately known. This is why I will punish you for all your crimes" (Amos 3:2, CJB). With opportunity comes responsibility.

So, the Feast is important. Responding to the invitation is crucial. What does that have to do with us?

We Get to Deliver the Invitations

Yeshua's Parable of the Great Banquet tells us that the God of Israel appoints people like us to deliver his invitation to others. From the beginning of the parable above:

> Once a man gave a banquet and invited
> many people. When the time came for
> the banquet, he sent his slave to tell those
> who had been invited, "Come! Everything
> is ready!" (Luke 14:16–17, CJB)

Each of us is the slave mentioned in this parable. You could say that the guest list is so large that God has had to divide up among his servants the task of encouraging people to respond to the invitation. Paul speaks of this division of duties more than once. In his letter to the Galatians he says that Cephas (Peter), James, and John (the Jerusalem group) were designated to invite

Jews to the banquet, and Paul himself, to invite the Gentiles.

In Romans 11, Paul underscores this differentiated guest list, using the metaphor of two fullnesses—the fullness of Israel (the full number of Jews to be at the God-Feast) and the fullness of the Gentiles (the full number of people from the nations to be at the Feast). All have their role to play in filling the seats at the Great Feast God is preparing. These are two distinct but related guest lists. What this means is that Jews don't have to become Gentiles, nor do Gentiles have to become Jews, in order to find their place at the table.

Historically, the summons to go and invite the Gentile world to God's banquet is called "the Great Commission." The church is used to thinking of the Great Commission as its "marching orders." These were the last words Yeshua gave to his disciples before he ascended to the Father's throne. That gives them unique weight. But the Bible never uses the term "Great Commission." The term "great" is a judgment call by which Christianity has ranked this commission as "great."

In a way, there can be no argument on the matter. Certainly this is *a* great commission that has informed and spurred heroic service for nearly two millennia. But let's remember the term doesn't come from Scripture and is actually quite recent. The first person to use the term was probably Dutch missionary Justinian von Welz (1621–1668). And it wasn't until the nineteenth century that James Hudson Taylor, the founder of the

China Inland Mission, popularized the term and connected it with the Gospel of Matthew 28:19–20.

But what about that other fullness, that other guest list, coordinate with but different from the fullness of the Gentiles? What about the fullness of Israel? Paul shares a discovery that astounds him. It should grab us too:

> But if their transgression means riches for the world, and their loss [most of Israel declining the invitation to embrace Yeshua as the Messiah] means riches for the Gentiles, how much greater riches will their full inclusion bring! ...For if their rejection brought reconciliation to the world, what will their acceptance be but life from the dead?
> (Romans 11:12,15, NIV)

Paul calls Israel's eventual mass accepting of the invitation "much greater riches" than the fullness of the Gentiles. He says this is because this fullness triggers "life from the dead," what theologians call "the general resurrection," when the dead who are part of the guest list will be raised in embodied immortality. This is when the party without compare, God's Great Feast, can really begin. That's why it's "much greater riches," and why it is fair to call the summons to gather Jewish people to the Great God-Feast, "the Greater Commission."

So What?

It is nice to know about these extraordinary future events. But Scripture doesn't prophesy things in order to satisfy our curiosity or to thrill us with some inside scoop. God wants us to align ourselves with what he will be doing, to prepare for it, and even to hasten events through our cooperation.

We can see this clearly in 2 Peter 3:11–14 where Paul talks about the eventual end of the world as we have known it, and the creation of a new heaven and a new earth (the habitation of the redeemed of all the ages). But in view of all this, Peter asks us, what kind of people should we be? He says we should lead holy and godly lives, waiting for and hastening these events. Here then is the pattern—prophesied events, big ones! But we are told of them in order to eagerly anticipate them and to also support them through our own efforts.

Since we've just been told that the fulfilling the Great Commission is important, and fulfilling the Greater Commission even more important, what does this have to do with us now? I have a suggestion.

Members of the fullness of the Gentiles should primarily busy themselves with helping others like them find their way to the table, while Jewish Yeshua-believers are especially equipped and called to do all we can to remind our people to respond to God's RSVP. We should especially be engaged in serving the

Greater Commission by extending the invitation to our own people. Remember, the Master of the Feast sends his slave(s) to tell those who had been invited, "Come! Everything is ready!" God is sending us to deliver the invitation!

Some Complaints About the Guest List

Some people resent this differentiated guest list. It is common these days to think of all people as being alike, and that therefore there should be only one great guest list. Some don't like the idea of differentiation, period! The idea that Jews should continue to live as Jews, while Gentiles have their own God-given cultural contexts annoys those who believe that being one big, happy family requires that we all be the same.

They seem to think that Yeshua came to make us equal by making us uniform. But what about those of us who differentiate? What about those who don't want to embrace a theology of the homogenized people of God?

Lots of people have no problem with this idea. They think it makes for peace and equality. They even enlist the aid of the Bible to prove their point, exploring two Pauline metaphors—the One New Man and the Olive Tree. They say these passages teach equality through uniformity—a homogenized people of God. Let's see if they're right.

Does the One New Man Point to Uniformity Among the People of God?

Let's look first at the One New Man. It's a term Paul uses in Ephesians Chapter 2 to express how it is no longer true, as in ancient times, that Gentiles and Jews are destined to live at enmity with each other, in fact, always defining themselves as opposites. Of course we agree that because of what Messiah has done, the Jewish and Gentile worlds are now reconciled to each other in the Messiah.

But then people take the idea further, insisting that Paul is saying Jews and Gentiles are now the same! This is where people make an interpretive mistake. Paul is talking about unity, while these people are talking about uniformity. Those are two very different things!

Paul makes it clear that being equal does not mean being the same. The equality he speaks of has no pecking order, no hierarchy, no disparity of status. What critics don't grasp is that this should not be taken to mean that there is no distinction!

Instead, Paul means that in the Messiah's community, Jews and Gentiles may all now live together in peace, as he says, "For he is our peace, he who made both one and broke down the dividing wall of enmity, through his flesh" (Eph 2:14, NABRE). The word "both" acknowledges the continuing "two-ness" of the Jews and the Gentiles as the people of God in Messiah, who has made the two (that remain two) into one (meaning these two groups now live together in unity).

To help us understand that he is talking about unity in diversity, Paul writes in Ephesians 3:6, "through the gospel the Gentiles are fellow heirs, fellow members of the body, and fellow partakers of the promise" (NET). To be fellow heirs, fellow members, and fellow partakers means there must be another partner with whom these Gentiles are joined, that is, the Jews. What we have then is unity (not uniformity) amidst diversity/duality.

It helps to zero in on three words: unanimity, uniformity, and unity. Unanimity means being in complete agreement, and uniformity means being completely alike. Neither of those are God's way of dealing with things. God is into unity, which means living together in peace and harmony while distinctions or differences remain in place. This is the miracle God performed for two communities that historically always rejected the other in defining themselves. No more of this! Now it is unity amidst diversity, and diversity amidst unity.

Let's turn now to that other Pauline metaphor that is commonly abused and misused—the Olive Tree.

Does the Olive Tree Point to Uniformity Among the People of God?

The answer is "No." Simply paying attention to the context and the details of the metaphor, we can see that the tree does not represent the uniformity of the people of God, but rather the tree represents a unity amidst difference.

The tree represents the whole people of God. The root of the tree is God's covenantal relationship with his people, beginning with Abraham, Isaac, and Jacob (and Sarah, Rebecca, Rachel, and Leah). That is a unity. But the tree has both Jewish and Gentile branches that remain differentiated throughout the metaphor!

In verse 14, we read, "And if the root is holy, so are the branches." The root of God's people, his covenantal purposes and promises, is holy, and so are the branches, the people of God in their unity and diversity. Unity because they are all in the same olive tree; diversity, because throughout his metaphor there are natural branches (Jews), and wild branches (the other nations, that is, the Gentiles).

Paul never ignores the differentiation between the two, and they do not become three or more kinds of branches. Paul describes two kinds of branches which ever and always remain two—the Jewish branches and the Gentile branches, both resident in the same olive tree.

Paul says, "some of the [Jewish] branches were broken off, and you—a wild olive—were grafted in among them and have become equal sharers in the rich root of the olive tree" (Rom 11:17, CJB). Notice Paul's careful terminology: Even when grafted into the olive tree, Gentiles remain wild branches "grafted in among them." Who is "them"? The Jews, whom Paul terms "the natural branches."

Paul warns the Gentiles in verses 17–18 not to boast against the natural branches, but to remember that it is the root, the covenants of God which were made with the patriarchs and matriarchs of Israel, that supports the Gentile branches. This can only mean that the Gentiles should see themselves as dependent upon the covenants God made with the Jewish people. The Gentiles are honored guests in a Jewish home, and Paul insists they must never forget to honor their Jewish hosts.

As we read the rest of Paul's olive tree allegory, we discover something else: The Jews, even when broken off, are still called natural branches. And the Gentiles, even when grafted into the olive tree, still remain wild branches. This preserves what Paul wishes to preserve—the differentiation between Jews and Gentiles, natural and wild branches. And let's not forget: It is not a distinction of status, but it is an enduring distinction.

Despite the clear evidence of such texts and the rational way they fit together, some people will not accept what is taught here about a unity that preserves and celebrates diversity. Nevertheless, Paul does a great job making his point. I invite you to join me in agreeing with him!

Giving This Legs

We have seen that God has committed to us, his servants, the task of inviting others to his Great Feast. In his parable about that Feast, Yeshua reminds us that there will be some people at the table whom we might not expect to be there and whom we would never have invited, while there will be others, ideal for the Feast, whose failure to respond to the RSVP leaves them outsiders to the Feast, leaving us sad and frustrated.

In keeping with Paul's teaching about the fullness of the Gentiles and the fullness of Israel, linked to the Great Commission and the Greater Commission, it is logical that we who are Jews have a special responsibility to invite others of our people to the Feast. The fancy term for that assignment is that it is our "mission," (the Hebrew term would be *sh'lichut*). Similarly, in general, the church world should be occupying itself with delivering invitations to the nations, expediting the Great Commission, the fullness of the Gentiles.

However, we Jews ought not to be indifferent to the progress of the fullness of the nations, nor should the church world be indifferent to the progress of the fullness of Israel. Why? Because it is only when both fullnesses are accomplished that the Great Feast begins, including the resurrected dead on the guest list! Wow!

Think of it like any other feast. While the food is great to eat, and the camaraderie around the table is a source of deep delight, we need to remember it took a lot of hard work to get the food ready, the guests there, and everything just right. What does this mean for us? Just this! We all have work to do. In Chapter Four we learned all about how to invite people. Let's do it!

B'teiavon! Hearty appetite!

FOR BETTER DIGESTION

1. In his first letter to the Yeshua-believers in Corinth, Paul refers to Jewish and Gentile identities as "callings," meaning that each group has particular responsibilities. How do you think this might apply? Or does it?

2. Which do you think is more reasonable in today's society: To say that all people are really the same, or to say that while people are different, they can and should live together in peace and harmony?

3. Is there anything about Paul's two fullnesses that surprises you?

4. How might people improve in how they respond to differentness?

MORE FOOD FOR THOUGHT

Stuart Dauermann, *Christians and Jews Together*

In this brief monograph, I lay out the nature of the Great Commission and Greater Commission and their implications for the responsibilities of Israel and the *ekklesia* from among the nations. This is a detailed exploration of Romans Chapter 11.

Mark S. Kinzer and Jennifer M. Rosner, ed., *Israel's Messiah and the People of God: A Vision for Messianic Jewish Covenant Fidelity*

Mark Kinzer is the premier Messianic Jewish theologian in the world. A marvelous thinker and writer, his books are must-haves for anyone serious about Messianic Judaism and its future. And Jen Rosner is one of the very top thinkers and scholars in the field. If you want to understand why Jews who believe in Yeshua should live a Jewish life, this book is what you want to read. Somewhat sophisticated but never pretentious, and always clear.

Mark S. Kinzer and Christoph Schönborn, *Searching Her Own Mystery: Nostra Aetate, the Jewish People, and the Identity of the Church*

Mark Kinzer is one of the few Messianic Jewish leaders whose breadth of thought and experience qualifies him to speak with equal authority to Orthodox, Roman Catholic, and Protestant Christians, and to Messianic Jews in a variety of contexts. Here he addresses the Roman Catholic Church, calling it to go ever deeper into the implications of the Church's advances in its relationship with the Jewish people since Vatican II. His coauthor is a highly respected and brilliant Roman Catholic Cardinal noted for his interfaith work.

Mark S. Kinzer, *Postmissionary Messianic Judaism: Re-defining Christian Engagement with the Jewish People*

This was Mark's first book on Messianic Judaism. It presents a holistic picture of Messianic Jewish identity, theology, and practice. It is a must-read for anyone interested in the nature and future of Messianic Judaism. People who consider themselves thinkers will have difficulty setting it down. Bravo.

Mark S. Kinzer, *Jerusalem Crucified, Jerusalem Risen: The Resurrected Messiah, The Jewish People, and the Land of Promise*

Kinzer's masterful analysis of the theological intent and design of Luke-Acts demonstrates conclusively the deep significance of seeing Yeshua of Nazareth as the one-man Israel, a title attached to him by Jewish scholar Will Herberg. You will see how what happens to Yeshua as the crucified and the risen and reigning Messiah will also happen to his people Israel, crucified, risen, and reigning. A remarkable exegetical achievement.

Mark S. Kinzer and Russell L. Resnik, *Besorah: The Resurrection of Jerusalem and the Healing of a Fractured Gospel*

This recasting of the material found in *Jerusalem Crucified* makes its wisdom accessible to a wider audience.

TAKE-OUT

God views Jews to be natural branches of his saving purposes in the world. How then shall we live?

CHAPTER SEVEN

LIGHT THE LAMPS! THE SPIRIT OF THE FEAST

In this chapter we'll be considering the deepest satisfaction in human life—experiencing and interfacing with the Presence of God. Nothing stands ahead of this. But first, a story.

Long ago in a galaxy far away, I was on the road with a music group. Traveling from city to city, most often we ate our meals with host families. To paraphrase Henry Wadsworth Longfellow, "When it was good it was very, very good, but when it was bad it was horrid!"

The worst times were when we stayed with people who only offered to put us up out of duty. Even if the home was expensive and the food good, when the vibes were chilly, it was always awkward at best, and we were eager to move on. On the other hand, even the most humble of meals in an unimpressive home amidst warm hosts was like an oasis in our desert of constant travel.

The same is true when talking about the spiritual "meals" in this book. It is the spirit, or in this case the Spirit (the Divine Presence), that makes all the difference. Otherwise, it's just details and more details. Because the difference between spiritual warmth and mere mechanics is so important, in this chapter we'll take a look at the light, the life, and the pizzazz that brings life to our practices and our gatherings. Take time to think and pray about the Spirit of God.

Yeshua Points Us to the Presence of the Spirit

At that meal we call "The Last Supper," Yeshua talked about the Spirit of the Feast. Always the master teacher, Yeshua connects the meal they are eating that night with the Great God-Feast yet to come:

> "I have really wanted so much to celebrate this Seder with you before I die! For I tell you, it is certain that I will not celebrate it again until it is given its full meaning in the Kingdom of God." Then, taking a cup of wine, he made the *b'rakhah* and said, "Take this and share it among yourselves. For I tell you that from now on, I will not drink the 'fruit of the vine' until the Kingdom of God comes."
> (Lk 22:15–18, CJB)

In a sense this Last Supper was just the hors d'oeuvre pointing to the coming Feast. And it was at this meal that Yeshua delivered his final briefing preparing the Twelve—and us—to live rightly as we await his return and the banquet. And beyond that, he shares with us the resources we will need to get there in style.

Enter the *Ruach HaKodesh*— The Divine Presence

We find the notes from this meeting gathered together for us in John's *Besorah* (The Gospel of John), chapters 13 to 17. There we learn that Yeshua promised a remarkable intimacy with himself through his Spirit whom he was going to be sending to be with them forever. He described this as a kind of a union between them and the Divine Being. And he explicitly includes us in the equation, when he prays this to the Father:

> I pray not only for these [the disciples at
> the Last Supper], but also for those who
> will trust in me because of their word, that
> they may all be one. Just as you, Father,
> are united with me and I with you, I pray
> that they may be united with us, so that
> the world may believe that you sent me.
> The glory which you have given to me, I
> have given to them; so that they may be
> one, just as we are one—I united with
> them and you with me, so that they may
> be completely one, and the world thus re-
> alize that you sent me, and that you have
> loved them just as you have loved me.
> (John 17:20–23, CJB, brackets added)

When we read that, we should all do a double take. This is beyond extraordinary. Yeshua is praying for us that we might experience a union with the Father comparable to that which he himself experienced. This is so extraordinary that many people miss it. But there it is. Reread the text. Just thinking about it bends the mind.

In this orientation seminar, Yeshua prepared his followers for the transition between having him with them and knowing he is gone. He tells them, "Where I am going, you cannot follow me now; but you will follow later" (John 13:36, CJB).

We are living in a different kind of transition than they were. Our transition is between this age and the Age to Come (see Eph 1:21). Now that Yeshua has died and risen, ascending to the Father from where he poured forth the Divine Presence, the Age to Come and the Present Age are overlapping. Theologians call this living between the already and the not-yet. We are experiencing a foretaste, but not the fullness, of the Age to Come, the Age of the Spirit.

Think of it like a vestibule of the Age to Come, getting a whiff of the Age to Come, and even having appetizers brought out to us preparing us for being seated at the Great God-Feast.

This is the Age of the Spirit. The writer of the Letter to the Hebrews reminds us that we have already experienced the powers of the Age to Come (see Heb 6:5), and Paul says we are those "upon whom the end of the ages has come" (1 Cor 10:11, RSV).

Yeshua briefs us in the Upper Room discourse at the Last Supper, telling us how the coming of the Spirit has extraordinary implications for us as we live in this age, while having been invaded by the powers of the Age to Come. This is what is known as "inaugurated eschatology." The great biblical theologian George Eldon Ladd taught us to reframe our thinking, so that we would see that we are living our lives between the already and the not-yet. We are already experiencing the Age of the Spirit, the first fruits of the Age to Come, even though it is not yet here in its fullness. Yeshua tells the disciples and us that after his resurrection, he will be sending his Spirit to be with them, and with us, forever. Think about that for a moment. Then think again.

The Age of the Spirit is how God's entire agenda for Israel and the nations moves into hyper-drive. There has been a great shift in God's order of things, and we are supposed to get fully involved with it. On that very special *Shavuot*, known by Christians as the Day of Pentecost, Peter connected this to the resurrection and ascension of Yeshua: "He has been exalted to the right hand of God; has received from the Father what he promised, namely, the *Ruach HaKodesh*; and has poured out this gift, which you are both seeing and hearing" (Acts 2:33, CJB).

The Spirit has already been poured out. But we are not yet at the consummation of all things. We are living between the already and the not-yet. Don't judge how extraordinary this is by the tepid responses that surround us all. This is revolutionary and all-encompassing and worth everything we are and have.

Look at it this way. As heirs of the Spirit, we are living between D-Day and V-Day, two milestones in WWII.

D-Day, June 6, 1944, was when the forces of the Allies landed at Normandy. When that happened, the eventual vanquishing of the Nazi beast was assured. That day guaranteed ultimate victory, although the War wasn't over for almost a year. It wasn't until V-Day, May 8, 1945, that victory in the war in Europe would be declared.

In Yeshua's great battle with the forces of darkness in this present evil age, we are living between D-Day and V-Day, the already and the not-yet. Yeshua's death, resurrection, ascension, and pouring out of the Spirit is D-Day. The defeat of the forces of darkness, sin, death, and decay is guaranteed. But as with WWII, we are left with a mopping-up operation. Our not-yet V-Day won't arrive until Yeshua returns. In the meantime, God supplies us with the resources of the Spirit, experiencing a foretaste of the Age to Come.

And this coming of the Spirit is detectable. It is not meant to be just a doctrine but an experienced reality—"what you now see and hear" (Acts 2:33, NIV).

Stuart Dauermann

The Divine Presence as an Experienced Reality, Even for Us

Scripture repeatedly portrays the coming of the Spirit as life-giving and transformational. The Older Testament foreshadows it, and it comes into fuller bloom in the Newer Testament. Still, the implications of the sending forth of the Spirit remain out of focus for many Yeshua-believers. Let's adjust our lenses and bring all of this back into focus now. Let's begin with the Older Testament.

The Presence of the Spirit in the Older Testament

Samuel was an early and pivotal prophet in the history of Israel. He was the one whom God used to anoint with oil, and therefore authorize, Israel's first two kings, Saul and David. This anointing with oil was symbolic of being empowered by the Divine Presence.

When Samuel anoints Saul to be Israel's first king, he tells him where to go from there and mentions some people he will meet along the way. But notice what he says about what will happen at that encounter:

> "You will meet a group of prophets coming
> down from the high place, preceded by
> lutes, tambourines, flutes and lyres; and
> they will be prophesying [speaking in a
> manner that betokens the Presence of the
> Spirit]. Then the Spirit of ADONAI will fall

167

on you; you will prophesy with them and
be turned into another man! When these
signs come over you, just do whatever you
feel like doing, because God is with you.
Then you are to go down ahead of me to
Gilgal, and there I will come down to you
to offer burnt offerings and present sacrifices as peace offerings. Wait there seven
days, until I come to you and tell you what
to do." As it happened, as soon as he had
turned his back to leave Sh'mu'el, God
gave him another heart; and all those
signs took place that day.
(1 Sam 10:5–9, CJB, brackets added)

Earlier, while Israel was in the wilderness, something similar occurred. Moses felt he needed a cadre of
people to share with him the burdens of leading Israel.
God answered by directing him to select seventy leaders whom God would equip to help Moses lead the
people. Here is the account of what happened. Notice
what it says about the Spirit, and about what Moses
wished for that day:

Then he collected seventy of the leaders
of the people and placed them all around
the tent. ADONAI came down in the cloud,
spoke to him, took some of the Spirit that
was on him and put it on the seventy lead-

ers. When the Spirit came to rest on them, they prophesied—then but not afterwards.

There were two men who stayed in the camp, one named Eldad and the other Medad, and the Spirit came to rest on them. They were among those listed to go out to the tent, but they hadn't done so, and they prophesied in the camp. A young man ran and told Moshe, "Eldad and Medad are prophesying in the camp!" Y'hoshua, the son of Nun, who from his youth up had been Moshe's assistant, answered, "My lord, Moshe, stop them!" But Moshe replied, "Are you so zealous to protect me? **I wish all of A**DONAI**'s people were prophets! I wish A**DONAI **would put his Spirit on all of them!**" (Nu 11:24–29, CJB, emphasis mine)

We are living in the day when God is responding to this wish, this prayer of Moses. Now is the time when the Divine Spirit is poured out on all of ADONAI's people.

The Presence of the Spirit in the Newer Testament

In Acts Chapter 2, fifty days after the crucifixion of Yeshua, the Divine Presence came upon his follow-ers like a mighty rushing wind, and crowds gathered,

attracted by the clamor. Many assumed Yeshua's followers were all drunk because they saw them strongly
affected by the Spirit and heard them speaking in languages they had never learned (quite a manifestation)!
Peter explains:

> "These people aren't drunk, as you sup-
> pose—it's only nine in the morning. No,
> this is what was spoken about through the
> prophet Yo'el:

> 'ADONAI says:
> "In the Last Days,
> I will pour out from my Spirit upon everyone.
> Your sons and daughters will prophesy,
> your young men will see visions,
> your old men will dream dreams.
> Even on my slaves, both men and women,
> will I pour out from my Spirit in those days;
> and they will prophesy."'"
> (Acts 2:15–18, CJB)

Moses had expressed his wish that the Spirit would
rest on all Israel. The prophets later predicted it. Here is
just one example:

> But now hear, O Jacob my servant, Israel
> whom I have chosen! Thus says the LORD
> who made you, who formed you from

the womb and will help you: Fear not, O
Jacob my servant, Jeshurun whom I have
chosen. For I will pour water on the thirsty
land, and streams on the dry ground; I will
pour my Spirit upon your offspring, and
my blessing on your descendants.
(Isa 44:1–3, ESV)

And through Yeshua it all came to pass.

More than once, Yeshua called this experienced reality of the Spirit "living water," the opposite of stagnant
water. This is water on the move, pure and life-giving.
He further says, "If anyone is thirsty, let him keep coming to me and drinking! Whoever puts his trust in me, as
the Scripture says, rivers of living water will flow from
his inmost being!" (John 7:38, CJB). Notice what he says
about the scope of this promise. It is for *whoever* trusts
in him, and it is no trickle of the Spirit, no *shpritz*. It is
rivers of living water flowing out of our inmost being.
Does it get any better than this? If this is not promising
an experiential reality, I don't know what is!

Peter amplifies the universal availability of this resource for all of Yeshua's people when he says:

Turn from sin, return to God, and each
of you be immersed on the authority of
Yeshua the Messiah into forgiveness of
your sins, and you will receive the gift of
the *Ruach HaKodesh!* For the promise is

for you, for your children, and for those
far away—as many as ADONAI our God may
call!
(Acts 2:37–38, CJB)

Notice—for you, for your children, for those who
are far away, as many as ADONAI our God may call. The
promise is universal for all of Yeshua's people!

This was an old promise, of which the proph-
ets spoke extensively. It is not just a fulfilled promise,
though. It is a gift. Peter says "the *gift* is for you and
your children." Yeshua also refers to the Presence of
the Spirit as "a gift," saying: "if you, even though you are
bad, know how to give your children gifts that are good,
how much more will the Father keep giving the *Ruach
HaKodesh* from heaven to those who keep asking him!"
(Luke 11:13, CJB).

So, we are talking about a promise, a gift, something given to all of Yeshua's people, something for
which we should be continually asking, a reality from
which we are meant to drink deeply. Radical transformation. Who would say no?

The Divine Presence: Who Needs It?

Scripture makes clear that without this dynamism,
something vital is missing. This must be what happened in Acts 19, when Paul arrived in Ephesus and
was met by twelve disciples but detected something
was not quite right. Notice the question Paul asks them,

and ask yourself, "What prompted him to ask that unusual question?"

> While Apollos was in Corinth, Sha'ul
> completed his travels through the inland
> country and arrived at Ephesus, where
> he found a few *talmidim*. He asked them,
> "Did you receive the *Ruach HaKodesh*
> when you came to trust?" "No," they said
> to him, "we have never even heard that
> there is such a thing as the *Ruach Ha-
> Kodesh.*"

> "In that case," he said, "into what were you
> immersed?" "The immersion of Yochanan,"
> they answered. Sha'ul said, "Yochanan
> practiced an immersion in connection
> with turning from sin to God; but he told
> the people to put their trust in the one
> who would come after him, that is, in
> Yeshua." On hearing this, they were im-
> mersed into the name of the Lord Yeshua;
> and when Sha'ul placed his hands on
> them, the *Ruach HaKodesh* came upon
> them; so that they began speaking in
> tongues and prophesying. In all, there
> were about twelve of these men.
> (Acts 19:1-7, CJB)

Apparently, Paul noticed there was something about these disciples that didn't quite ring true. They seemed to be missing something—that is, the *Ruach HaKodesh*. Notice that Paul considers the coming of the Spirit to be crucial—not an added frill, but standard equipment! That is why he immerses them in Yeshua's Name and lays hands on them and "the *Ruach Ha-Kodesh* came upon them; so that they began speaking in tongues and prophesying." Again, as is often the case with the coming of the Spirit, there is a transformation of the speaking faculties: prophetic speech—weighty words from God—and sometimes speaking in tongues.

Some will argue that this is a narrative passage and that therefore one cannot draw authoritative teaching from it. That's an important issue, and worth considering. But for the time being, notice two things. First, in both Testaments, God instructs his people through narrative stories, from the very first page—the story of creation—to the last, the story of the new creation. And far removed from dismissing narrative as a source of divine guidance, Paul himself writes that "All Scripture is God-breathed and is valuable for teaching the truth, convicting of sin, correcting faults and training in right living; thus anyone who belongs to God may be fully equipped for every good work" (2 Tim 3:16–17, CJB). Certainly that includes the narratives, from which Paul himself derived spiritual teaching, as in 1 Corinthians 10:1–10.

Of course, we know that Paul was one of the major crafters of how Yeshua-faith was to be lived out this side of the Resurrection. That's why we mustn't miss how he himself stresses this coming of the Spirit as a life-giving transformative reality. For him this is nonnegotiable and something to be assumed as the norm. In one of his earliest letters, to Galatia (in modern Turkey), he asks his disciples, "I want to know from you just this one thing: did you receive the Spirit by legalistic observance of Torah commands or by trusting in what you heard and being faithful to it?" (Gal 3:2, CJB). He is referring to receiving the Spirit as something he could point back to as a recognizable event they all shared. And he asks them how *that* (the coming of the Spirit) happened for them. It was memorable experiential reality, or he could not refer to it as a memorable "that."

In his Second Letter to the Corinthians (in modern Greece), he describes this encounter with the Spirit in a rich cluster of terms: "Moreover, it is God who sets both us and you in firm union with the Messiah; he has anointed us, put his seal on us, and given us his Spirit in our hearts as a guarantee for the future" (2 Cor 1:21–22, CJB). This is an elegant passage showing the respective interactive roles of the Father, the Son-Messiah, and the Spirit, seen here as the element of anointing, as a seal, as a gift in our innermost being (our hearts), and as a guarantee. Quite rich and worth mulling over.

Paul calls the Presence of the spirit a "guarantee." When you have a guarantee, you already have something which points toward something greater that you will have later. The Greek term here is *arabon,* which is also translated "earnest" or "down-payment."

Paul uses this term to indicate that the Corinthians are already experiencing something which serves to assure them of a greater something coming in the future. So, let's get clear on the main point: The prevailing assumption in the Newer Testament is that the coming of the Spirit is an experienced reality.

Let's all be careful not to react to these things passively, taking all of this for granted, something to be checked off on a list. No. Scripture admonishes us to be active seekers of the Spirit in all his fullness, and to be radically engaged so as to face dramatic new possibilities. That is why Yeshua can say, "If anyone is thirsty, let him keep coming to me and drinking" (John 7:37, CJB), and "how much more will the Father keep giving the *Ruach HaKodesh* from heaven *to those who keep asking him!*" (Lk 11:13, CJB, italics added). And on the Day of Pentecost, the crowds realized that the coming of the Spirit called for a response on their part, which is why they said "Brothers, what shall we do?" (Acts 2:37, NIV).

These are strange new things, I know. Let's see how Scripture helps us to actively seek the Presence of the Spirit in our lives. Look at it in these ways:

1. **The *Ruach* Present**—The Spirit of God is present throughout all of creation (the common word is "omnipresent"). We see this from the very beginning of

the Bible: "In the beginning God created the heavens and the earth. The earth was unformed and void, darkness was on the face of the deep, and the Spirit of God hovered over the surface of the water" (Gen 1:1–2, CJB). The Spirit is always and everywhere present. David contemplates that, saying. "Where can I go to escape your Spirit? Where can I flee from your presence? If I climb up to heaven, you are there; if I lie down in Sh'ol, you are there" (Ps 139:7–8, CJB). This is the Spirit conceived of spatially in relation to everything in the time-space continuum—omnipresence.

2. **The *Ruach* Prior**—This is the Spirit at work in our lives even before we knew it. When we look back over how we got to a spiritual breakthrough, just about all of us who have come to Yeshua-faith can see how God was drawing and preparing us for that outcome long before we were aware it was happening. This is the *Ruach* Prior. Yeshua put it this way: "No one can come to me unless the Father—the One who sent me—draws him" (John 6:44, CJB).

It is the work of this *Ruach* Prior that takes us when we are still very wet behind the ears and immerses us into the supernatural realities that await us. So, Paul says, "It was by one Spirit that we were all immersed into one body, whether Jews or Gentiles, slaves or free; and we were all given the one Spirit to drink" (1 Cor 12:13, CJB).

3. **The *Ruach* Within**—This is the Spirit alive in us. The Spirit that hovered over creation, the Spirit that

drew us and immersed us into one body, one diverse faith community—the Spirit which we were given to drink, the actual Spirit of Messiah, His essential self—that Spirit lives inside of us. There are many passages that speak of this deep, exciting, and significant reality and it takes a long time to explore and get seated in this massive paradigm shift. But just look at this startling passage, for instance:

> But you, you do not identify with your
> old nature but with the Spirit—provided
> the Spirit of God is living inside you, for
> anyone who doesn't have the Spirit of the
> Messiah doesn't belong to him. However,
> if the Messiah is in you, then, on the one
> hand, the body is dead because of sin;
> but, on the other hand, the Spirit is giving
> life because God considers you righteous.
> And if the Spirit of the One who raised
> Yeshua from the dead is living in you, then
> the One who raised the Messiah Yeshua
> from the dead will also give life to your
> mortal bodies through his Spirit living in
> you.
> (Rom 8:9–11, CJB)

Go ahead: Read that three times slowly. Then try to wrap your mind around what it says. It's all rather amazing, but this is at the heart of what has happened for us, to us, and in us through what Messiah accomplished. And at the very least, this opens to us new vistas of intimate relationship with God, experiencing and interacting with the *Ruach* Within. This includes:

a. The Spirit's work regenerating us—making us spiritually alive to God in ways we didn't know before.
b. The *Ruach* illuminating God's truth so that it comes alive for us in new ways. So it is that in the Upper Room Discourse, the Messiah tells his disciples, "the Counselor, the *Ruach HaKodesh*, whom the Father will send in my name, will teach you everything; that is, he will remind you of everything I have said to you" (John 14:26, CJB).
c. The Fruit of the Spirit, a Spirit-energized renovation of our character, so that we increasingly reflect the *Tzelem Elokim*—the Divine Image. We read of this in Galatians, chapter five:

> But the fruit of the Spirit is love, joy,
> peace, patience, kindness, goodness,
> faithfulness, humility, self control.
> Nothing in the Torah stands against such
> things. Moreover, those who belong to
> the Messiah Yeshua have put their old
> nature to death on the stake, along with its
> passions and desires. Since it is through
> the Spirit that we have Life, let it also be
> through the Spirit that we order our lives

day by day. Let us not become conceited,
provoking and envying each other.
(Gal 5:22–26, CJB)

4. **The *Ruach* Upon**—As we have seen in the account of King Saul's early experiences, and that of the seventy elders whom God empowered to work with Moses, the Older Testament shows foregleams of the Spirit coming upon people to enhance their abilities. For example, when the Tabernacle in the wilderness was being built (a multi-roomed tent with ornate furnishings, prior to the time of the Temple), the Divine Presence filled Bezalel the artisan with wisdom, understanding, and knowledge in how to work with various media. The same is true of other artisans involved in the project (see Ex 31:1–11, CJB). And then of course the Spirit also fortified Samson with supernatural strength. We all know something of that story! (See Judg 14.)

Sometimes Scripture speaks of the Spirit clothing people (the Hebrew root is *labash*), but we could argue that actually it is the Spirit who is clothed with the people! The Spirit so inhabits the people that, for a brief time, the *Ruach* wears the people like a garment. This Hebrew verb for "clothing" is used of the Spirit in Judges 6:34, in 1 Chronicles 12:18, and in 2 Chronicles 24:20.

Notice how different translators translate the verb. Some say the Spirit of God took control of someone, or clothed someone, or came on/upon someone, or took possession of someone, or enveloped him or her. How-ever, the idea of the Spirit either clothing the person, or even the Spirit putting on the person as a garment is the most interesting for us. It shows that the Divine Presence wants to have an intimate partnership with us.

These incidents in the Older Testament were sit-uational and episodic, reserved for special people performing special roles at special times. The phenom-enon came and went in different circumstances. But since the Day of Pentecost, when the *Ruach* was poured out, the Spirit endues all of God's people.

Another verb used to describe this reality is *tza-lach*, usually translated as "rush/rushed upon." The Spirit is perceived to be rushing upon someone. This may be phenomenological language, describing the sensations experienced at such a time. Again, the verb is used episodically—the Spirit does this for a purpose and at certain times. This is not something ongoing, but occasional.

So, we read: "The LORD's spirit empowered him [Samson] and he tore the lion in two with his bare hands as easily as one would tear a young goat" (Judg 14:6, NET); and again, "The LORD's spirit empowered him. He went down to Ashkelon and murdered thirty men" (Judg 14:19, NET); or of Saul when Samuel anoints him: "Then the spirit of the LORD will rush upon you and you will prophesy with them. You will be changed into a different person" (1 Sam 10:6, NET); and later in that chapter, "When Saul and his servant arrived at Gibeah, a company of prophets was coming out to meet him. Then the spirit of God rushed upon Saul and he prophesied among them" (1 Sam 10:10, NET).

But this phenomenon should be more frequent and more widely distributed in our day, not less so, because we are living this side of the resurrection, the ascension of Messiah, and the consequent outpouring of the Spirit. We are experiencing a foretaste of the Age to Come, the Age of the Spirit.

While we have Older Testament precedents for leaders and key figures having dramatic encounters with the Spirit, because we are now living in the Age of the Spirit, these dramatic encounters and empowerments are available to all of us. This is the new normal for the people of God.

5. **The *Ruach* Among**—The promised gift of the Spirit is not a private affair. It cannot be limited to the individual's experience. In fact, the Presence of the promised Spirit functions especially as a gift to the community of God's people. The Spirit transforms our relationships, also transfusing and transforming our gathered worship. At least this is the way it is supposed to be. This will then result in a certain beauty and boldness in how we interface with the wider world.

The Spirit comes among us, bestowing gifts of enhanced abilities to bring spiritual growth and benefit for the sake of the community. Paul tells how, in the gathered assembly, "to each person is given the particular manifestation of the Spirit that will be for the common good" (1 Cor 12:7, CJB).

Paul connects this with the resurrection of our Messiah, saying,

> Each one of us, however, has been given grace to be measured by the Messiah's bounty. This is why it says,

> "After he went up into the heights, he led captivity captive and he gave gifts to mankind." (Eph 4:7–8, CJB)

Tying This All Together

We have seen therefore these five dimensions, five arenas where the Divine Presence operates, bringing blessing and enrichment:

The *Ruach* Present

The *Ruach* Prior

The *Ruach* Within

The *Ruach* Upon

The *Ruach* Among

So much more remains to be said in each of these areas, but our intention has already been met—to present an introductory overview. Despite the limitations of our information thus far, here are some suggestions for more deeply experiencing the benefits we have been examining together.

- **Thirst**—Yeshua said, "Whoever puts his trust in me, as the Scripture says, rivers of living water will flow from his inmost being." This promise of the *Ruach* applies to all of us. So pray that God will make you really thirsty for what he wants to give you. Pray for thirst.

- **Repent**—That is, reconsider whether your way of living has been toward God or away from him. Has it been an effort at obedience or an expression of autonomy? Do your attitudes toward God's truth and his authority in your life, as well as about the claims of Yeshua, need to be revised in your life? How? When?

- **Be immersed**—Fully identify with Yeshua, who in his death and resurrection so fully identified with all of us.

- **Surrender**—Present yourself to God as his servant. Turn over the keys to the car of your life.

- **Desire**—Intensely desire a greater depth of encounter/experience with and usefulness to the *Ruach HaKodesh*, this sense of conjoined being, such that you might be clothed with the *Ruach* and the *Ruach* might clothe himself with you.

- **Ask**—Always be asking God for the Spirit that he promised.

- **Believe**—Believe that you have obtained what you asked for, because that's the kind of God we have. And after all, he promised.

• **Influence**—In the community setting where you nurture your Yeshua-faith, see what influence you can be in encouraging learning and experimentation in the areas we have outlined here.

FOR BETTER DIGESTION

1. We learned of five avenues of the Presence of the *Ruach*. The first was "The *Ruach* Present." What are the others?

2. You will find that some people avoid speaking of the role of the *Ruach* in our lives because they associate the subject with weirdness. Do you think the *Ruach* and weirdness necessarily go together?

3. What are some ways to avoid going overboard in matters of the Spirit?

4. How do you feel and think about seeking to live in partnership with the Presence of the *Ruach*?

MORE FOOD FOR THOUGHT

Jack Deere, *Why I Am Still Surprised by the Power of the Spirit: Discovering How God Speaks and Heals Today*
This is a substantial rewrite of a book that first appeared in the 1990s. The author, a former Associate Professor of Old Testament at Dallas Seminary, went through a massive paradigm shift in his attitudes and practices concerning the immanence of the Divine

Presence. While there are anecdotes in this book, its great strength is Deere's deep acquaintance with the biblical text. This is a great book for the curious and the unconvinced, as well as for the persuaded. Not to be missed.

Gordon D. Fee, *God's Empowering Presence: The Holy Spirit in the Letters of Paul*

Dr. Fee, likely his generation's premier Pauline scholar, addresses every text in the Pauline letters that refers to the Holy Spirit. Somewhat technical, but still quite readable, this is a must-have for those who love Paul, the Holy Spirit, and both combined.

Gordon D. Fee, *Paul, the Spirit, and the People of God*

Eminently readable summary of *God's Empowering Presence*. More accessible and a delight to read. Get it!

Craig S. Keener, *Three Crucial Questions about the Holy Spirit*

Craig Keener is one of the world's premier New Testament textual scholars. Author of more than 30 books, his writings are renowned for his depth of research. He also has some experience with the Messianic Jewish world. This book provides foundational understandings to help us make room for an interactive and balanced relationship with the Divine Presence.

Craig S. Keener, *Gift and Giver: The Holy Spirit for Today*

This book is somewhat autobiographical. This is a revision of the 2000 edition. It is the best work in print to reliably introduce readers to the array of giftings the Holy Spirit brings.

David Martyn Lloyd-Jones and Christopher Catherwood, *Joy Unspeakable: Power & Renewal in the Holy Spirit*

I was so startled by this book that after reading it once, I then read it again. Martyn Lloyd-Jones was a very conservative Bible teacher, world-renowned, and a preacher whose power came not from style, but from a meticulous handling of the text. Somehow his meticulous examination of the text of Scripture deeply affected people. But because he was so careful and deliberate, he was the last person I expected to speak and teach about the power of the Holy Spirit. I was wrong. Anyone who respects Scripture is likely to be as convinced as I was by Lloyd-Jones's argument for a work of the Spirit in our hearts and lives separate from simply coming to faith in Yeshua. Perhaps his meticulous care is in part due to Lloyd-Jones having been a medical doctor prior to becoming a preacher.

Philip J. Noordmans, *FireStarter: The Holy Spirit Empowers*

I have met the author and his wife, unpretentious people of God. At that time, he was pastoring a largely Chinese church in California. The book is well-reasoned, balanced, and convincing. Carefully done without a syllable of hype.

Jackie Pullinger and Andrew Quicke, *Chasing the Dragon: One Woman's Struggle Against the Darkness of Hong Kong's Drug Dens*

Jackie's story and the impact of her life are unforgettable. Trained as an oboist, in her early twenties, she went off to China with a few pounds sterling in her purse, believing that somehow God wanted her there. Her powerful ministry to prostitutes, drug addicts, and gangsters is unforgettable evidence that the Spirit that raised Yeshua from the dead has not retired. The book is fascinating and inspiring. She has lived in Hong Kong for more than fifty years and is deeply respected there for her lifetime of service to the community.

TAKE-OUT

We were never meant to simply believe the right things without experiencing the touch of God on our lives. So let's pay attention to both areas as we continue our journey with the Jewish Jesus.

CHAPTER EIGHT

KASHRUT: MEALTIME MINDFULNESS, JEWISH-STYLE

Let's talk about what you eat. Yes, really.

You are probably thinking that what you eat is nobody else's business. I get it. But as MOTs (Members of the Tribe), we ought to reconsider. It seems God has a diet plan. And trust me, although it may not subdue our waistlines, his program just may service our souls.

This dietary program is called *kashrut*, "the body of Jewish dietary law."[1] But why this preoccupation with food?

This should come as no surprise. After all, wasn't the first commandment God gave to people about food? Remember this one? "You may freely eat from every tree in the garden except the tree of the knowledge of good and evil. You are not to eat from it, because on the day that you eat from it, it will become certain that you will die" (Gen 2:16–17, CJB).

Perhaps the reason for this preoccupation with food is that no issue is more regarded as nobody else's business than the question of what we choose to put in our mouths. You can test this out yourself by going up to someone while they are eating and saying, "Do you think you should eat that?" Let me know how it goes!

Here's the point. The command to abstain from eating of the tree of the knowledge of good and evil in the Garden was not so much about food as it was about relationship. It was a test to see if Adam and Chava (Eve) would respect God's right to regulate their lives. They failed the test, and most of us Jews do as well, three times a day, every day, not counting snacks! We all fail the test of letting God intrude upon our personal space in *every* area of life. And that includes what we eat.

But look at things from the positive side.

Every time we eat within his guidelines, we identify as God's servants. We take a stand for being Jews; we serve as a link between past and future generations. We say a very Jewish "Yes" to God. In a world where everyone is talking about their rights, we recognize that God has rights too, even the right to tell us what to eat and when.

Kosher eating is an ideological signpost signifying that humankind is not meant to be a melting pot, but rather, a salad. Gentiles remain Gentiles, and Jews remain "A people dwelling alone, Not reckoning itself among the nations" (Nu 23:9, NKJV). And part of that dwelling apart is that we eat differently from others. By eating kosher, we stand apart and we stand together. And four millennia of Jewish survival prove that's a good idea.

Before sketching out the outlines of *kashrut*, we should heed these warnings: First, *kashrut* is not about dietary perfectionism. None of us should be looking over our shoulder for the food police to write us up for doing it all wrong, spelling out which ordinance we transgressed.

Avoid those folks. While God is perfect, he is no perfectionist, and he's not a nag. Don't let holy umpires harass you, and don't become one yourself. Avoid becoming overscrupulous. It's exhausting going through life counting jots and tittles. Don't go there.

And second, while *kashrut* can be demanding and difficult, it is not stupid. You will see that there is a reason for everything—reasons that keep God in mind.

Let's take a look at *kashrut*, God's Jewish diet plan!

You Don't Have to Be Buddhist to Be Mindful

Kashrut is about mindfulness. For example, it reminds us of who we are. Jewish food practices are part of the holy etiquette God gave so Jewish people could honor him as a kingdom of priests and a holy nation. Maintaining this link honors the covenantal unity Jews share across the generations. For sure, eating kosher isn't going to win heaven for you. It doesn't get you "a ticket to ride." Instead, it's a way of showing respect for God and a way of remaining connected to other Jews across time. And that's good enough. It keeps us mindful of who we are.

191

Let's talk about some other ways that eating kosher is about mindfulness.

Kashrut trains us to be mindful of the particular kind of food we are eating. That's why we say a different blessing for different kinds of foods. We also avoid eating certain foods altogether and eating milk products and meat together. These guidelines remind us that God created everything "according to its kind." If God made a difference in creating, we should make a difference in consuming.

See, for example, Genesis 1:25—"God made each kind of wild beast, each kind of livestock and every kind of animal that crawls along the ground; and God saw that it was good." And also, of plants—"God said, 'Let the earth put forth grass, seed-producing plants, and fruit trees, each yielding its own kind of seed-bearing fruit, on the earth'; and that is how it was. The earth brought forth grass, plants each yielding its own kind of seed, and trees each producing its own kind of seed-bearing fruit; and God saw that it was good" (Gen 1:11–12, CJB).

Judaism is mindfulness genius. While of course, Jews believe in keeping God's commandments, the tradition insists we do it mindfully, with *kavvana,* meaning "with intention, sincere feeling, attentively, and with a focused heart and mind." It's never sufficient to just "go through the motions." Judaism spurs us to self-awareness, communal awareness, and God-awareness in the details of holy obedience.

First, we cultivate mindfulness through the blessings we say. We create mindfulness through the statements we make just prior to performing a ritual act or some mundane experience which we wish to elevate in our consciousness and the world. These statements are *b'rakhot*—blessings.

Maybe you think it strange to imagine that words elevate something spiritually, but this is a common fact of life. The fancy term for the kind of speech that changes the status of something just by being uttered is "performative speech." In Jewish life, when a groom gives an object of acknowledged worth to a bride in the presence of witnesses and says, *"Harei at mekudeshet li b'tabaat zu k'dat Moshe v'Yisrael,* (Behold you are consecrated unto me with this ring in accordance with the law of Moses and [the People of] Israel)," this act and these words make them husband and wife. Or when the rabbi or minister at a wedding says, "I now pronounce you man and wife," his words change their status. This is performative speech—speaking the words changes status.

The Newer Testament validates all of this where Paul writes to his protégé Timothy, "everything created by God is good, and nothing received with thanksgiving needs to be rejected, because the word of God and prayer make it holy" (1 Tim 4:4–5, CJB).

So, let's get down to the business of eating.

What are the blessings our tradition teaches us to say? There are five different ones, and we choose different ones depending upon what food we are dealing with.

All of these blessings start the same way: *Baruch ata* Aᴅᴏɴᴀɪ, *Elohenu melech ha-olam*, meaning, "Blessed are you O Lᴏʀᴅ, our God, King of the universe." After that comes a closing phrase which is different for each of five categories of food. Here are the blessings:

1. There's one for any meal that includes bread made from any of five grains found in Israel (wheat, rye, oats, barley, or spelt). We finish the blessing by saying: *hamotzi lechem min ha-aretz* (who brings forth bread from the earth). Colloquially, we refer to this blessing as the *motzi*.

2. The one for a snack including another grain product, but not the five grains mentioned above, starts the same way and ends with the words *borei minei mezono* (who creates various kinds of substances).

3. One blessing is for eating vegetables and all foods that grow in the ground: *borei p'rei ha'adama* (who creates the fruit of the ground).

4. Another blessing is for fruits and all foods that grow on trees: *borei p'ri ha'etz* (who creates the fruit of the tree).

5. And one blessing is for milk, meat, fish, eggs, liquids, candies, and other categories not covered previously: *she-ha-kol nihiyah b'dvaro* (by whose words all things came to be).

Don't worry: You don't say a blessing for all of these foods at the same meal! You say a blessing over the predominant food at the meal, and when a meal includes bread, then just say the *motzi*. That blessing over the predominant food, or, when appropriate, over bread, covers the entire meal.

Learning these *b'rakhot* will take you maybe a few weeks. Deciding which blessing to say is a small thing that makes a big difference. Every time you eat is an occasion to elevate your mindfulness by asking and answering, "What do I have before me here? What am I thanking God for?" And having said our brief blessing, we then just eat and enjoy!

But let's be clear: This is not dead ritual unless we do it mindlessly. If things are dead, it is not the ritual's fault, it is our fault. Jewish life rejects mindlessness. We strive to do everything with *kavvana*, with intentionality, directionality, and mindfulness.

Second, we cultivate mindfulness of what we may and may not eat. We all know that for Jews, some foods are disallowed. We learn to avoid them out of respect for God and to mark us as a people set apart for his service, joined to other Jews in a common way of life. You may have been told these food guidelines were instituted for health reasons. Not true. The only reason certain foods are not allowed is because we believe God said so!

While *kashrut* originated in the Bible (see Leviticus 11 and Deuteronomy 14), Jewish communities have standardized, interpreted, expanded, and explained them for centuries.

Here are some of the basics. Don't get overwhelmed. This is for your information:

- To qualify as kosher, mammals must have split hooves and chew their cud.

- Fish must have fins and removable scales.

- Only certain birds are kosher. Birds of prey are not kosher.

- All of this means pork, rabbit, eagle, owl, hawks, buzzards, catfish, sturgeon, shellfish, and reptiles, among others, are nonkosher.

- Nearly all insects are nonkosher, although there are a small number of kosher locust species.

- Meat and dairy products should not be cooked or consumed together.

- A kosher food becomes nonkosher if processed or cooked with a nonkosher food or element.

- And as we shall see, kosher species of meat and fowl must be ritually slaughtered in a prescribed manner to be kosher. This is because Judaism is very sensitive to the suffering of living things.

Third, we cultivate mindfulness of the health and condition of the animals we consume. One of the terms for nonkosher is *tref* (sometimes spelled *treif*) which means "torn," referencing Exodus 22:31 about not eating animals that are torn in the field, that is, animals that had been attacked by one or more other animals and left dead. Such animals were not to be eaten. From this reference, Jewish practice developed a category of damaged animals that similarly were to be considered *tref*, or nonkosher. This includes animals with certain bodily defects, and also those with lesions, lacerations, broken limbs, missing or punctured organs, or bodily damage due to attack by another animal.

In recent years, some religious Jewish authorities have become concerned for the health of the lungs of the animal in question, with the gold standard being animals with smooth lungs rather than lungs having any puncture or adhesions of certain kinds. The term in Yiddish for "smooth" is "*glatt*." Kosher animals that have been especially inspected for the health and integrity of their lungs are termed *glatt kosher*.

Yes, all of this may seem like TMI, Too Much Information. But it's always good to be informed. And some of us will want to walk this more exacting path.

Before we raise our eyebrows about all this punctiliousness, we should realize that these practices connect us to how things were done in the Temple, where respect for God dictated that only unblemished animals could be offered to him. It was a sign of respect for the God of Israel that we would sacrifice to him only the best and most perfect specimens from our flocks and herds. To this day, our eating at meals is a priestly act, something we do in the presence of God to bring him honor.

We see the opposite of this respect in the Book of Malachi, which critiques the attitudes and behaviors of priests who couldn't be bothered with such things:

> "A son honors his father and a servant his master. But if I'm a father, where is the honor due me? and if I'm a master, where is the respect due me?—says ADONAI-Tzva'ot to you *cohanim* who despise my name. You ask, 'How are we despising your name?' By offering polluted food on my altar! Now you ask, 'How are we polluting you?' By saying that the table of ADONAI doesn't deserve respect; so that there's nothing wrong with offering a blind animal as a sacrifice, nothing wrong with offering an animal that's lame or sick. Try offering such an animal to your governor, and see if he will be pleased with you! Would he even receive you?" asks ADONAI-Tzva'ot.
> (Mal 1:6–8, CJB)

Fourth, we cultivate mindfulness of how animals were slaughtered. Our tradition insists that animals must not be subjected to needless suffering. This is the principle, *tza'ar ba'alei chayim* (the suffering of living creatures). While not explicitly written in the Torah, this prohibition is extrapolated from the biblical law requiring us to assist in unloading burdens from animals (see Exodus 23:5).

Sensitivity to animal suffering extends to regulating the ways in which animals are killed, an area known in Judaism as *shechitah*. In Jewish law, animals are killed by having their throats cut swiftly with a blade that must be very sharp and without even a nick in the blade in order that the stroke might be swift and unimpeded. Such a stroke causes the animal's blood pressure to immediately reduce, reducing consciousness and pain.

If you find this subject unpleasant, believe me, I get it! But these are facts of life—and death—in a world where not everyone is a vegan or a vegetarian.

Fifth, we cultivate mindfulness by ecological awareness. The principle of not being needlessly destructive to the created order is *bal tashchit* (do not destroy). It is rooted in a fascinating passage in Deuteronomy 20:19–20, which forbids the armies of Israel from cutting down fruit trees to use the wood to make siege-works in times of war. The wording in verse 19 is quite striking: "When, in making war against a town in order to capture it, you lay siege to it for a long time, you are not to destroy its trees, cutting them down with an axe. You can eat their fruit, so don't cut them down. After all, are the trees in the field human beings, so that you have to besiege them too?" (CJB). How fascinating to see this ancient document discussing the moral rights of trees!

Jewish practice extends this principle to include other forms of senseless and unnecessary waste and destruction. Adequate cause must be found before destroying or depleting natural resources. *Bal tashchit* is the foundation of Jewish environmental activism.

Sixth, we are mindful of how meals are prepared. Generally, this means we do not cook our foods on Shabbat, we do not serve or prepare milk and meat together, and we do not adulterate our foods using nonkosher ingredients of any kind, such as a food coloring made from shellfish.

Seventh, we are mindful of what may be eaten with what. Three times in the Torah we find this mysterious statement: "You are not to boil a young goat (or a young animal) in its mother's milk" (Exod 23:19; Exod 34:26; Deut 14:21). The Torah gives us no reason for this prohibition. Some authorities suggest it is either to prevent the moral trespass of heartlessly boiling a baby animal in the milk of its mother, or perhaps, that it refers to a pagan fertility rite.

Judaism strives to obey God, even in cases where his will on a matter is not clear. To keep from violating this commandment about not boiling a kid in its mother's milk, the tradition builds a fence around the prohibition, making it wider than it was. This provides a safety margin to prevent violating a command where the rationale is not explicit. Therefore, as a precaution against boiling a kid in its mother's milk, Jews do not even mix dairy and meat food products. Observant

Jews do not eat milk and meat together and will wait either three or six hours (according to custom) between eating a meat meal and a dairy meal.

Religious Jews also use separate dishes and implements for meat and dairy foods and will prepare them in separate utensils. Glass dishes are exempt since they can be thoroughly washed so that any vestiges of milk or meat are gone. Glass dishes can be used both for a meat meal and a dairy meal.

In this chapter, I certainly don't want to give you indigestion. We're not going to tell you everything you ever wanted to know about *kashrut* but were afraid to ask, or worse, everything you didn't care to know about *kashrut* and didn't care to ask. This book is meant to provide the first word on the subjects we cover, not the last word. It is all about overview. Nobody is forcing anything on you. And you can go as fast or as slow, as far or as near, as you wish. But these are holy pathways, worthy of our respect.

Before we finish this detailed chapter, it will pay off if we make things more approachable. So, come along and meet our Ladder of Observance.

The Ladder of Observance for Growing in Kashrut

After millennia of experience, the Jewish community has learned that people do not go directly from nonobservance to observance. All of us are people in process, and each of us changes at our own rate of speed. It is not so important how far along the road we are—it's more important that we are on a good road and heading in the right direction!

The road of Jewish observance is sometimes thought of as a ladder. And some in the Jewish community speak of growing in Jewish observance as climbing a ladder. This concept is explained in a book by Rabbi Bradley Shavit-Artson, *It's a Mitzvah! Step-by-Step to Jewish Living*. The ladder begins with the easiest and most basic of practices, and gradually "ascends" step by step through more demanding practices.

Individuals will stay on one rung or another for different lengths of time until they are ready to climb higher, if at all. So don't be in a hurry, don't let anyone push you, and don't for a moment imagine that you must reach the twelfth rung, or that you need to get there as fast as possible, or it's just no good even trying. That has nothing to do with observance, and everything to do with being obsessive-compulsive! Don't bother with that!

So here we go. We are starting from the easiest rung—on the ladder, the lowest rung—toward the highest.

1. Abstain from all pig products.

2. Refrain from eating shellfish such as lobster, shrimp, oysters, and mussels.

3. Eat only kosher varieties of fish. The biblical in-junction is that only fish with fins and scales may be eaten.

4. Separate milk products from meat products in cooking and eating.

5. Observe at least a minimal waiting period between eating a meat meal and any dairy product. (Most people wait three hours; the more scrupulous wait six hours.) There need not be a waiting period af-ter a dairy meal. Before starting to eat meat, how-ever, it is traditional to rinse our hands with water as a way of removing any stray cheese (or ice cream!) left behind from a prior meal. And if you are sitting at a table, clear away the dairy foods as well as the utensils and plates that were used with them before presenting the meat meal.

6. Learn to look at the labels of foods you purchase to see if they are kosher.

7. Avoid using eggs that contain any blood. My grand-mother did this by holding eggs up to a candle to see if there was a spot within the shell. Easier to do, whenever preparing an egg dish, first crack open the eggs in a glass bowl to see if there is any blood in the eggs.

8. Eat only biblically permitted meat, conforming to the guidelines given in Leviticus 11 and Deuteron-omy 14.

9. Acquire dishes to use only for dairy and *pareve* (neutral—not meat or dairy—that is, vegan) meals. One set of glass dishes will work for all three categories.

10. Eat only meats that are certified as kosher. Start off doing this first at home, and then in the outside world.

11. Acquire kosher dishes, silverware, and pots for meat dishes. Glass dishes for all varieties of food are acceptable. Otherwise, yes, observant Jews actually have three sets of dishes—one set for meat, another for dairy, and a third for Passover—dishes that have never had contact with leaven. But again, ONE set of glass dishes works in all of the categories!

12. Practice the biblical tradition of "taking the hallah."[2]

A Word About Being Biblically Kosher

In and around the ranks of Jews who believe in Yeshua/Jesus, there are some who refer to being "biblically kosher." What do we mean by being "biblically kosher?" This means to only observe kosher restrictions explicitly stated in the Torah, and to not bother with or be restricted by rabbinic interpretations of right practice, or traditional standards.

I identify two problems with this approach. First, never in the history of the world has there been a Jewish community that took this stance about *kashrut*. Even the Karaites, a small Jewish sect that does not accept Rabbinic tradition, has its own oral law, its own traditions, about matters such as how to kill an animal for eating, and, for example, whether one may kill a pregnant animal. Rabbinic Judaism says "Yes," and Karaites, "No." Torah's laws of *kashrut* were given to the Jewish people as a transgenerational covenant community and not to us as individuals. Because this is so, right standards and interpretation were, and remain as, matters to be decided by the Jewish community to whom Torah was given.

Whenever such discussions take place, what emerges is a kind of oral law, and the seeds of the development of a communal tradition. In other words, the laws of Torah, including the food laws, never existed apart from a community that asked and discussed, "Just how are we going to do this?" This is unavoidable. There is nothing extraneous or intrusive about such a process. It is both normal and necessary. Choosing instead to be biblically kosher means to repudiate the Jewish religious tradition and its exemplars. It means opting instead for an individualist approach to Jewish practice. It is the religious equivalent of everyone doing his or her own thing. It separates us from our history and from our people. And it is based on the fallacy that God gave us a book, and not a communal way of life with all the processes entailed. Not good.

Second, being biblically kosher is impossible because the written Torah leaves gaps in our knowledge, thus preventing us from following its written commands until those gaps are filled. Here is just one example. We are told in Torah, "If the place he chooses to locate his name is too far for you, *you may slaughter any of your herd and flock he has given you just as I have stipulated;* you may eat them in your villages just as you wish" (Deut 12:21, NET, italics added). Here we are told that God stipulated how the animals were to be slaughtered, but nowhere in the Torah or in the *Tanach* as a whole are we told what this manner of slaughter is. Therefore, our tradition has extrapolated what that instruction might be, and it has done so respectfully and with due gravity, since what we are dealing with here is the will of God and what to do about it.

When the Torah tells us (Lev 20:14) to take together four species on the first day of Sukkot, which four species are meant, and what are we supposed to do with them? The Jewish tradition discusses this, and we need the assistance it provides! The Torah tells us not to do any *m'lakha*, commonly translated as "work" on Shabbat, without ever defining for us what the *m'lakha* exactly is which we are to refrain from doing on that day.

So, it seems clear that an oral tradition is inevitable and necessary even if we wanted to content ourselves with being "biblically kosher." We cannot be biblically kosher apart from resorting to an oral tradition of explanation as to what that means and how it is done. The explanations we give will either be our own, or of our own congregation, or that of the Jewish tradition. In my view, since Yeshua-believing Jews are already viewed to be ignorant and rejectionist about Jewish religious life, it is a good idea to adhere to normative Jewish standards whenever possible rather than inventing standards of our own. Inventing our own makes it seem that we are rejecting Jewish life and community in order to form separate communities of our own. Not a good idea.

Before You Leave the Table, Remember to Say "Thank You!"

Years ago, I heard a Christian seminary professor share a story that makes a Jewish point.

Once he spoke at a church meeting and received a lunch invitation from one of the church members. When they sat at the table, the food was served, and contrary to what he was used to, no thanks were given to God at the beginning of the meal.

The host then asked the seminary professor if he had noticed that no thanks (saying grace before the meal) were given, to which the professor said, "Why yes, I did notice that."

The host went on to explain why this was the case. "We are not hypocrites here, Professor. We don't thank God for the food because it was not God, but I myself who worked hard and earned the money to bring the food to the table."

The Professor was shocked, because he remembered something that this host had managed to conveniently forget. In the Torah it is written, "You will think to yourself, 'My own power and the strength of my own hand have gotten me this wealth.' No, you are to remember ADONAI your God, because it is he who is giving you the power to get wealth" (Deut 8:17–18, CJB).

This story and the Torah text remind us to not forget the thanks that we owe God, especially when we are busy being impressed with ourselves!

Birkat HaMazon

Fortunately, the Jewish tradition supplies a practice. It is a block of praises to God called "*Birkat HaMazon.*" If you're just not ready for a bunch of details right now, even interesting details, then you can skip over this section. But do get to it sometime. This IS interesting stuff. And the practice itself will enrich you.

The practice of reciting and singing *Birkat HaMazon* is founded on a text found just a few verses away from the one we just quoted. It says, "So you will eat and be satisfied, and you will bless ADONAI your God for the good land he has given you" (Deut 8:10, CJB). Go ahead and eat! Enjoy yourself! But then say "Thank you" to the God from whom all good things come!

It's all about mindfulness again. Just as we elevate our awareness through deciding what *b'rakha* (blessing) to say at the beginning of the meal, so at the end of the meal, we say blessings to elevate our awareness of the goodness of God in the past, praying that he would continue extending that goodness into the present and future for ourselves, our people, and our world. Jewish history reminds us that we are good at forgetting. This tradition counteracts that flaw.

These blessings are musically fun, but also theologically rich. The *Birkat HaMazon* is an artistically woven theology of Divine Providence, God's watchfulness over creation. Once you get past the initial learning curve of this practice, you will marvel at its artistry.

The Structure of *Birkat HaMazon*

As an introduction to the prayer, we sing a psalm, and there are a wide range of beautiful melodies to help us do this. On weekdays it's Psalm 137, *al naharot bavel* ("By the Rivers of Babylon"). Checking YouTube, you will find quite a few versions, including those by Don McLean and Boney M., as well as various Hebrew versions. There was even a song based on this text in the show and movie *Godspell*. We read, chant, or sing this Psalm to remember that even in times of joy and relaxation, like eating a meal with friends and family, we mourn the destruction of Jerusalem and the Temple and our consequent exile.

We remember that life is good, but sometimes, times are bad. We honor God and our people by not forgetting.

On Shabbat and on festivals, we recite Psalm 126 instead. This Psalm looks forward optimistically to the restoration of Zion and Israel's consummation.

Then we come to the *Birkat HaMazon* proper. When three or more Jewish adults eat together, we begin with an introductory summons—an invitation to bless God. Commonly, the host or the most distinguished person present is given the honor of leading. If a *Kohen*, a member of the priestly family, is present, he or she will be given the honor. Then we come to an invitation for the group to join the leader in blessing God for the food, to which there is a response, and more responding by the leader until we get to the actual four blessings which each have a name, in case you care to know.

The first three blessings are regarded as required by scriptural law and the fourth one was added because our tradition thought it was a good idea.

1. *Birkat HaZan*—Blessing of thanks for the food. This is a public thanksgiving for God's goodness to humanity as a whole, celebrating the Creator and Sustainer of all.

2. *Birkat Ha'Aretz*—Blessing of thanks for the land of Israel. Here we move from God's goodness to all, to God's particular goodness toward the Jewish people. This benediction has two paragraphs:

a. *Nodeh lecha* offers thanks to God for all past favors granted to our people.

b. *V'al hakol* summarizes the previous blessings and ends with a *b'rakha*. On Hanukkah and Purim, minor holidays where God miraculously intervened, we add a short blessing called *al hanisim* ("For the Miracles"). And speaking of miracles, following the practice of Conservative Jews, at the right time of the year we insert another blessing for *Yom HaAtzma'ut* (Israeli Independence Day).

3. *Birkat Boneh Yerushalayim*—Blessing of thanks for Jerusalem. We celebrate our holy city and pray that it will be rebuilt to its former glory in our day. On Shabbat and other special occasions, there are brief inserts to acknowledge and give thanks for the occasion. Although without a doubt this will seem tedious to some, and can be made tedious by people who nag about such things, this attention to various benefits we have received is just another way of being mindful of God's many blessings to us. The tradition is reminding us to remember. And that's a good thing.

4. *Birkat HaTov v'ha-Meitiv*—Blessing of thanks for the One who is good and who does good—God himself!

The Jewish tradition is ancient. Over the centuries, our people have delighted in making additions to our prayers, including the *Birkat HaMazon*. That's why *Birkat HaMazon* includes a section of added one-sentence prayers all beginning with the word *HaRachaman* meaning "the Compassionate One," that is, God. For example, we pray that the Compassionate One will bless the host and those present, that He will hasten the coming of Elijah the prophet, and a prayer that we may be worthy to see the days of the Messiah. You can easily spot these prayers inserted into the texts of the *Birkat HaMazon* wherever you find them. And they are fun. You might even want to invent some *HaRachaman* prayers of your own.

The United Synagogue of Conservative Judaism has adopted a nice shortened version of the *Birkat HaMazon*, with additions in English, for general use in Conservative synagogues. It is also fun because of the great melodies used. And this shortened version, while still challenging, is not as arduous as the Orthodox version.

Let's Sing a Little!

On Shabbat there are lots of songs that we add to sweeten our time together. We supplement our feast of food with a feast of song. And that takes us to our next chapter on "Shabbat, Our Weekend Oasis." Read on!

FOR BETTER DIGESTION

1. What would you say to a Jewish Yeshua believer who told you, "I can't be bothered with following *kashrut*?"

2. Do other ethnic groups have their own food habits and traditional diets? Name some.

3. What steps might you take to increase Jewish awareness in your regular diet?

4. Does mindfulness increase or decrease life's satisfactions?

MORE FOOD FOR THOUGHT

https://ourrabbis.org/main/halakhah-mainmenu-26/kashrut-mainmenu-34

This material from the Messianic Jewish Rabbinical Council is the fruit of serious interaction with Jewish discussion on how best to honor the divine stipulations about Jewish eating. I recommend this material as a solid foundation which honors Scripture, tradition, Newer Testament realities, and the Lord of all.

https://ourrabbis.org/main/documents/MJRC_Standards_Aug2014.pdf

This is a full statement of Jewish standards of observance as developed by the Messianic Jewish Rabbinical Council. It is a document well worth your study and adherence.

TAKE-OUT

If it's a good idea to eat like a human being instead of like an animal, why might it be a good idea to eat like a Jew instead of otherwise?

CHAPTER NINE

SHABBAT: OUR WEEKEND OASIS

A Foretaste of the Age to Come

Look for a moment at this picture. It is not a painting, but a photograph. What is it?

Considering the barrenness and the heat of its surroundings, can you just imagine how fantastic it must feel to be crossing a desert inferno, struggling over countless dunes, only to see this? Incomparable!

It's an oasis. Here's an especially useful definition.

1. A fertile or green area in a desert or wasteland, made so by the presence of water.

2. A situation or place preserved from surrounding unpleasantness; a refuge.[1]

Notice that second definition, "a situation or place preserved from surrounding unpleasantness; a refuge." This is a perfect description of Shabbat, our oasis in the midst of time!

Shakespeare's Macbeth understood a major reason why we need this oasis.

> Tomorrow, and tomorrow, and tomorrow,
> Creeps in this petty pace from day to day,
> To the last syllable of recorded time;
> And all our yesterdays have lighted fools
> The way to dusty death.
> Out, out, brief candle!
> Life's but a walking shadow, a poor player,
> That struts and frets his hour upon the
>   stage,
> And then is heard no more. It is a tale
> Told by an idiot, full of sound and fury,
> Signifying nothing.[2]

Macbeth saw life as a deadly drudgery of meaningless monotony. A rat race. A treadmill that "creeps in this petty pace from day to day to the last syllable of recorded time." Shabbat comes to deliver us from this bondage, to sharply break the monotony, to give us our life back, an oasis rising in the desert. While many might view Shabbat negatively—a day that pulls us away from productive pursuits—others see things differently and more clearly.

In *The Gifts of the Jews: How a Tribe of Desert Nomads Changed the Way Everyone Thinks and Feels*, Thomas Cahill comments on Shabbat as the fourth commandment of the famous ten, highlighting how Shabbat breaks up Macbeth's dreaded monotony:

> No ancient society before the Jews had
> a day of rest. The God who made the
> universe and rested bids us to the same,
> calling us to a weekly restoration of prayer,
> study, and recreation (or re-creation).[3]

Cahill is reminding us that Shabbat is not just a time of cessation. It is not simply about subtraction. Shabbat is also about addition. Through prayer, study, and holy re-creation, it repairs us, restoring some measure of the wholeness that gets tattered and even lost in the day-to-day grind.

As the Shabbat *Birkat HaMazon* reminds us, Shabbat points us toward *hayom she-kulo Shabbat*, the day that is completely Shabbat (in the age to come). The author of the Book of Hebrews picks up on this metaphor, writing in chapter four that on the one hand, we have entered God's rest, but on the other, "there remains a Sabbath rest for the people of God" (Heb 4:9, ESV). For the recipients of the Letter to the Hebrews, as for us, Shabbat is an experience of "the already and the not-yet." And the already is meant to be a foretaste of the Age to Come (Heb 6:5).

Cahill also understands how Shabbat comes to remind Jews we are no longer slaves. Yet, even in the opulent West, some of us remain enslaved, especially to the pace of life and work, work, work. Which of us has not felt like just another cog in the wheel, a rat in the race. But the God of Israel had something else in mind for us:

> Leisure is appropriate to a free people,
> and this people so recently free find
> themselves quickly establishing this quiet
> weekly celebration of their freedom; lei-
> sure is the necessary ground of creativity,
> and a free people are free to imitate the
> creativity of God. The Sabbath is surely
> one of the simplest and sanest recom-
> mendations any god has ever made; and
> those who live without such septimanal
> punctuation are emptier and less re-
> sourceful.[4]

Each week we come to the Shabbat *oasis* to re-plenish the wellsprings of our body, mind, and soul, as members of the encampment of Israel crossing the wilderness of time on the way to our rendezvous with the Holy One. As the picture at the top of this chapter reminds us, an oasis is utterly different from all that surrounds it. This is the only way it can serve as a ref-uge from the surrounding unpleasantness. This is true of Shabbat as well; for it to do its job, it must be a differ-ent kind of day from all the others.

Not only do we want to preserve the Shabbat oasis from the creeping encroachment of the weekday wilderness, we also want to make room to intensify our attention to God, what nurtures our relationship with him, and what pleases him. We want to recuperate and be renewed.

We must be careful to not domesticate and secularize Shabbat. It is not simply a day of rest; it is a day of restoration. This is why Shabbat is a day especially given to God and in which we especially give ourselves to him. That some might think of this as boring only helps illustrate that we do not yet grasp the richness God has in store for us.

To make Shabbat happen, we need to get good at subtraction and addition. In the midst of the weekday wilderness, we will need to dig in and clear the space where the miracle of the Shabbat oasis can happen. And happen it will. So, hang in there. Later in this chapter we will talk about the great additions we can make to Shabbat. But before we get there, let's talk some more about clearing the space for the miracle to happen. Let's talk about subtraction.

The Big Subtraction: *M'lakha*

The Torah says Shabbat is a day for subtracting *m'lakha*. What is that? It's a nice-sounding Hebrew word. But there is just one problem: Nowhere in the Torah is it ever defined. Since giving God what he wants is Priority

#1 for them, religious Jews applied a lot of energy to discovering just exactly what *m'lakha* is.

The rabbis solved this conundrum by looking at the context of Torah's command, "On six days *m'lakha* is to be done, but the seventh day is to be holy for you, a Shabbat of complete rest in honor of Adonai. Whoever does any *m'lakha* on it is to be put to death" (Exod 35:2, CJB, modified). We find this verse just before Torah's extensive details about building the Tabernacle in the wilderness.

The Rabbis decided that *m'lakha* must be whatever activity was involved in the building of this Tabernacle. They extrapolated 39 categories of activity that went into building it plus hundreds of subcategories. For sure, this seems like overkill to us. We resist being required to do, or forbidden from doing, anything. But look at it this way: Extrapolating these categories was an exercise in respect and proper concern to do what God wanted. Again, you can't obey a command not to do X until you know what X is. This is the reason our tradition worked so hard at figuring out what *m'lakha* might be.

Ronald L. Eisenberg lists for us the categories of activity, the *m'lakha* forbidden to us on Shabbat:

> Activities that cannot be performed on the Sabbath are basic tasks connected with preparing the showbread (sowing, plowing, reaping, binding, threshing, winnow-

ing, selecting, grinding, sifting, kneading, baking), work related to making the coverings in the Tabernacle and the vestments used by the Kohanim [priests] (shearing [sheep], bleaching, carding [changing tangled or compressed material into separate fibers], dyeing, spinning, stretching [material], making two loops [meshes], threading needles, weaving, separating, tying [a knot], untying [a knot], sewing, tearing), activities concerned with writing and the preparation of parchment from animal skin (trapping or hunting, slaughtering, flaying [skinning], treating skins [curing hides], scraping pelts, marking out [to make ready for cutting], cutting [to shape], writing, erasing), construction (building, demolishing), kindling a flame (lighting, extinguishing), carrying (from private to public domain and vice versa), and putting the finishing touches to a piece of work already begun before the Sabbath.[5]

By eliminating these kinds of activities, we clear the radically different space that makes way for a transformative Shabbat. And that really is the point: putting up a stop sign before the ordinary that the extraordinary might come in.

221

There are other restrictions (subtractions) as well, also geared to create and to protect the specialness, the holiness of Shabbat. For those especially zealous to build an oasis, these are important too. Here are some of them. One must not do anything that (1) resembles a prohibited act or could be confused with it, to avoid setting a bad example for another Jew who will think they saw us performing the prohibited act; and, (2) one must not do an act that is linked with a prohibited act, or usually leads to performing a prohibited act.[6]

The rabbis are protecting us here from the impact of conditioned reflexes, recognizing that actions trigger other associated actions. Even if the actions performed would not normally in themselves be prohibited on Shabbat, they are traditionally disallowed to avoid triggering other behaviors that *are* explicitly forbidden.

Another Subtraction: They Call It *Muktzeh*

Going one small but significant step beyond what we have covered so far, our tradition also categorizes certain kinds of objects or activities as *muktzeh*, meaning "separated or set aside." Here we subtract using certain objects that were not "prepared" before the Sabbath. They are items which the vast majority of people would not expect to use or encounter on Shabbat. Such items and also some otherwise neutral behaviors, while not in themselves disallowed, should be avoided because they bring with them the atmosphere of the day-to-day

grind. Avoiding them helps to widen the boundary between the ordinariness of life and the specialness of
Shabbat. We leave them behind to wall off our oasis.
Even if you don't care to bother doing this, the logic is
sound and the effort, noble.

Such proscribed activities will include, for example,
packing suitcases, opening mail, discussing business,
preparing equipment for work, or organizing a brief-
case. The rabbis associate this precaution with an
admonition from the pen of Isaiah the Prophet highlighting excessive travel, pursuing the normal business
of life, doing one's usual things, and pursuing one's
interests. He speaks about them as corrosive to the
Shabbat oasis:

> If you hold back your foot on Shabbat
> from pursuing your own interests on my holy
> day;
> if you call Shabbat a delight,
> ADONAI's holy day, worth honoring;
> then honor it by not doing your usual things
> or pursuing your interests or speaking about
> them.
> If you do, you will find delight in ADONAI –
> I will make you ride on the heights of the land
> and feed you with the heritage of your
> ancestor Ya'akov,
> for the mouth of ADONAI has spoken.
> (Isa 58:13–14, CJB)

This passage shines a light on how the stipulations and prohibitions we have been discussing are not arbitrary. They are all calculated to perform the "magic" of clearing the ground and then creating and protecting an oasis, a weekly refuge, in the midst of time, a place where we find restoration and renewal, and where we touch the edge of God's Kingdom.

Yes, these restrictions are a hard sell nowadays. But if you pause to think about it, you will agree that your own experience proves how essential these measures really are. For example, think about a time when you were really fried, your life at school or at work had been hectic and brutal, and you swore to yourself that if you could just make it to the weekend, you were going to give yourself the kind of recovery time, perhaps some alone time, that you desperately needed. So, the weekend came. And then there was that call from a relative asking for a favor. There were other people who just wanted "a little of your time" for this, for that, for the other thing.

Your weekend got nickeled and dimed to death, and by Sunday night you were exhausted, upset, frustrated, and angry, swearing at yourself for blowing the weekend. How many times has this happened to you? And if you are a helpful kind of person, how does it make you feel when you are always up for grabs? Do you feel the frustration?

Now perhaps you can see the genius of Judaism's insistence on protecting the boundaries of Shabbat. If you don't clear the ground, build the special space, and jealously protect its boundaries, without any doubt the oasis will get away from you—or be taken from you.

So, let's look at another way of setting a boundary—carrying. Yes, simply carrying. This is another way of separating the Shabbat oasis from the day-to-day. If this is TMI, then skip this. But for the curious, here it is.

Yet Another Subtraction: Carrying

Building our personal Camp David for a meeting with God takes vigilance and effort. We have seen why the Jewish tradition is so attentive to preventing the climate and rhythms of daily life from encroaching on Shabbat. Another aspect of this boundary-setting is avoiding certain kinds of carrying.

The issue of carrying appears in two passages of Scripture. One is in the writings of Jeremiah the Prophet, who lived just before and during the beginning of the Babylonian Captivity in the sixth century BCE. This text comes from one of his sermons to a largely unresponsive population in Judah:

> Here is what ADONAI says: "If you value
> your lives, don't carry anything on Shab-
> bat or bring it in through the gates of
> Yerushalayim; don't carry anything out of

your houses on Shabbat; and don't do any
work *(m'lakha)*. Instead, make Shabbat a
holy day.
(Jer 17:21–22, CJB)

He warns against judgment ("if you value your
lives") and speaks against various kinds of commercial
or nonessential, mundane burden-bearing on Shabbat. Instead, they were to keep Shabbat holy—and that
means "set apart for God's special purposes." It was a
century before that when Isaiah adjured the people of
Judah to hold back from pursuing their own interests or
even speaking about them, as mentioned earlier. This
pursuing of one's own interests, this doing the usual
things, suggests the actions that Jeremiah later outlined (not carrying anything out of our houses and not
doing any work). Obviously, God wanted to keep the
Israelites home on Shabbat; he was serious about them
making a sharp break from the preoccupations of the
workaday world.

Of course, the Jewish community knows how, in
the modern world, this prohibition against carrying
outside of one's home might prove unduly burden-
some in practice. For this reason, the custodians of the
tradition made some accommodations, the chief one
being erecting something called an *eruv*. This is usually a wire strung around the perimeter of a Jewish area
which, for purposes of Jewish law (*halacha*), converts
the entire enclosed area to private space for each Jew

dwelling within the perimeter of the *eruv*. Since that space is now considered private, like one's home, restrictions against carrying on Shabbat no longer apply inside that perimeter.

Still Another Subtraction: Traveling

Toward further protecting the noncommercial character of Shabbat, traditional Judaism avoids travel on that day. The tradition also holds that driving a car violates Shabbat because of the sparks that are generated to burn the gasoline. This stricture is also true for electric cars because, with high-voltage circuits, a spark is created. This violates the prohibition against lighting a fire.

However, with modernity, life changes, and therefore, there are complications. One hundred years ago, Jews normally lived in Jewish districts and within walking distance of their houses of worship. With modernization and urbanization this is seldom the case, except in the case of practicing Orthodox Jews who take care to live in proximity to each other and to their synagogues. For this reason, the Conservative Movement allows driving so as to participate in worship services or to spend time with one's family, but not to go shopping. This is an accommodation to modernity.

Shabbat and Its Safety Valve: *Pikuach Nefesh*

Did you know that Jewish practice allows, even advocates, the violation of any Torah prohibition on the

Sabbath if a life is in danger or in potential danger? It does! This imperative to save a life, termed *pikuach nefesh*, supersedes all religious prohibitions except those against committing adultery, idolatry, and murder, which must never be countenanced under any circumstances.

The obligation to protect life prevails both in cases of immediate and less immediate threats to health or survival that might escalate. All of this is based on two verses in the Torah. "You are to observe my laws and rulings; if a person does them, he will have life through them; I am Adonai," and, "Do not go around spreading slander among your people, but also don't stand idly by when your neighbor's life is at stake; I am Adonai" (Lev 19:16, CJB).

Many in modern society, including those reflecting a certain consensus of Christendom, assume "the religion of the rabbis" is oppressive and unresponsive to human life and needs. This is a canard, "a groundless rumor or belief." Here are some sources from the heart of the Jewish tradition that refute this accusation. The first is a quote from the Babylonian Talmud:[7]

> One heats water for an ill person on Shabbat, whether to give him to drink or to wash him, since it might help him recover. And they did not say it is permitted to desecrate only the current Shabbat for him, but even a different, future Shabbat.

And one must not say: Let us wait and
perform this labor for him after Shabbat,
perhaps he will get well in the meantime.
Rather, one heats it for him immediately
*because any case of uncertainty concerning
a life-threatening situation overrides Shabbat.* And this is so not only with regard to
uncertainty whether his life is in danger
on the current Shabbat, but even in a case
of uncertainty with regard to danger on a
different Shabbat.
(TB, Yoma 84b)

Notice the clear reference to *pikuach nefesh*, the
overriding imperative to preserve life. And here is
another passage, from the teachings of the Rambam,
Rabbi Moshe ben Maimon, also known as Maimonides
(1135–1204), whose opinions are considered authoritative for all, and determinative for some:

These things [actions normally forbidden
on Shabbat] should not be performed by
non-Jews, minors, servants or women, lest
they consider the Sabbath a light matter;
instead, scholars and sages of Israel are to
carry them out. One must not put off the
desecration of the Sabbath in treating a
serious patient, as it is written: "If a man
obeys them he shall live by them" (Leviti-

cus 18:5), but he must not die by them.
From this you may infer that *the laws of
the Torah are not meant to wreak ven-
geance upon the world, but to bestow on it
mercy, kindliness, and peace.*
(Mishneh Torah, Shabbat 2:3)

Because the Rambam was a physician, it is natural that he would talk about a "seriously ill patient," but the principle he draws from Leviticus 18:5 is broader still. The laws of Torah are meant to be lifegiving, in his terms meant to "bestow...mercy, kindliness, and peace" on the world. That doesn't sound like oppressiveness to me! How about you?

Much more remains to be said on these matters, but not now, and not here. Remember our watchword: *Eat This Book!* is not meant to be the last word, but the first word, something to get you going, showing you a little bit of how and a lot of why.[8]

AT LAST!
WHAT SHABBAT ADDS TO OUR LIVES!

I promised you we'd get here, and even if your patience is running on fumes by now, here we are! Let's talk about what Shabbat adds to us. Then we'll talk about what we add to help build our Shabbat oasis.

What Shabbat Adds to Our Lives

Here is a principle to remember: *Shabbat adds to our lives what the pace and preoccupations of contemporary life take away.* This could be broken down into four areas: family, friends, food, and foundations. Let's look at these.

Family

I could *always* count on my friend Terry to talk to me about what was going on in her family. Even though she was single and had one brother and one sister, both a continent away, Terry was always full of news about them, about her Mom, and about her nieces, nephews, cousins, uncles, and aunts. She had stories from the past, and stories from the present. These conversations took place once or twice a month, and I loved it all. Why? Because warm family relationships are central to a rewarding life.

Another friend is Randy, a marriage and family therapist. His license plate says "1 of 5." Why? Because that is how he sees himself. With a wife and three daughters, Randy sees himself as 1 of 5, not as isolated but as part of a larger familial whole. He is relationally wealthy. No wonder he's a marriage and family therapist.

You've got your own stories, I am sure.

But such family relationships take time: and Shabbat gives us the gift of time to nurture those relationships. In part, Shabbat is about spending time with family. It is a good day for parents to be with their children, and children with their parents—a day for family members to not only be together, but to actually pay attention to one another, to talk, to play games perhaps, to have a face-to-face, rather than face-to-screen, relationship. And, although some religious Jews would frown on this, Shabbat is also a good time to call or visit family members located elsewhere, to check in with them, to strengthen family bonds.[9]

Because these are the people we are most apt to take for granted, family should have an honored and continual place in our weekly Shabbat observance.

For a good Shabbat, add family.

Friends

You would think that with our smartphones, iPads, and computers, and with applications like Facebook, we would be the most connected people in the history of humankind. This is not what we hear from Dr. Sherry Turkle of MIT. In three of her books, she has moved from exploring and informing about the interfacing of technology with human life and relationships, to sounding the alarm about how electronic media are warping how we relate to each other.

> Technology is seductive when what it offers meets our human vulnerabilities. And as it turns out, we are very vulnerable indeed. We are lonely but fearful of intimacy.

Digital connections and the sociable robot may offer the illusion of companionship without the demands of friendship. Our networked life allows us to hide from each other, even as we are tethered to each other. We'd rather text than talk.[10]

Many of us are finding that our world of relationships is ten miles wide and a half inch deep. Wouldn't it be wonderful to have one day a week to fast from social media and bask in actual face-to-face, in-the-same-room social contact? A day for meeting with friends, walking, talking, even studying texts together that take you deeper than Google or Facebook can provide? This is another gift Shabbat gives us—the return of our friends and of real face-to-face contact with them. Only when their presence is restored will we fully grasp what we lose by reducing friends and family to a Tweet or a screen image.

For a good Shabbat, add friends.

Food

Handling food on Shabbat is a bit tricky since we do what we can to avoid cooking on that day. Still, with a little bit of wisdom, it is amazing what you can do.

Here is the major trick when it comes to hot foods: While the tradition forbids cooking on Shabbat, that is, using heat to alter the chemical character of foods, once food is cooked it may be kept warm all day. So, cook food? No! Keep it hot all day? Yes!

In addition, you can use a slow cooker on Shabbat. It should be plugged in before Shabbat and the food at least half cooked before Shabbat arrives on Friday night. It then becomes a yummy resource for the following day. And for me? Make that a big slow cooker!

Religious Jews also use a device called a *blech* (and yes, it is a funny name). It is a metal sheet (usually aluminum or copper) that rests on top of the burners of one's stove, and in some cases also hides the knobs of the stove. With those burners on a low heat, the *blech* heats moderately, keeping warm whatever cooked goodies you have prepared for Shabbat.

Again, the reason we do not cook on Shabbat is that this is the one day a week when we do all we can to receive the day as given to us by God, without "monkeying" with it, without trying to put our creative mark on the created order. We endeavor to receive everything from the Creator of all.

The MJRC site includes this comment about why we do not cook on Shabbat:

> The traditional prohibition of cooking
> on Shabbat is implicit in the story of the
> manna (Exodus 16). The people gather
> two days' supply of manna each Friday,
> and prepare their Shabbat meals before
> the holy day begins: "This is what the

LORD has commanded: 'Tomorrow is a day of solemn rest, a holy Sabbath to the LORD; bake what you want to bake and boil what you want to boil, and all that is left over put aside to be kept until morning'" (Exod 16:23, CJB). The baking and boiling must be completed while Shabbat is still "tomorrow."[11]

For a good Shabbat, add food.

Foundations

After all we've covered in discussing Shabbat, it would be easy to get so wrapped up in constructing this oasis in time, this refuge of differentness, that we might forget that above all, this is a time to make room for encounters with God. For each and all of us, Shabbat should be a day when we get to study holy things more than on the other days of the week, especially to discuss these things with friends and family. It is also a day for expanded opportunities to pray. That, too, is good. So, Shabbat is not just a day for rest. It is a day for restoration, a day for renewal.

I remember hearing about a woman who did not bother going to her synagogue on Shabbat because she said, "Saturday is my Shabbat." Well, close but no cigar. It is not *your Shabbat*: it is *God's Shabbat*. In Leviticus 23 we read, "it is a Shabbat for ADONAI, even in your homes."

Perhaps we could take our cue from Tevye the Milkman who sang to us, "If I Were a Rich Man":

> If I were rich, I'd have the time that I lack
> To sit in the synagogue and pray.
> And maybe have a seat by the Eastern wall.
> And I'd discuss the holy books with the
>   learned men, several hours every day.
> That would be the sweetest thing of all.[12]

On Shabbat, every Jew is a rich man, a rich woman, a rich child. Shabbat is a foretaste of heaven. It involves more time to pray, more time to study holy things, and more time to do these things with others. Even though the song is not about Shabbat, it describes the bliss Shabbat brings. And every Shabbat, we can make it happen.

For a good Shabbat, add family, friends, food, and foundations—holy time, holy study, holy prayer.

You'll be as rich as Tevye ever dreamed.

FOR BETTER DIGESTION

1. What relationships and priorities in your life deserve a level of extra attention that other people might not understand?

2. Do you think Shabbat is worth the bother of subtracting and adding as this chapter suggests?

3. Do you agree or disagree with this statement, and why? "Just as doing something speaks of our priorities, so not doing something speaks of our priorities."

4. Pick two aspects of this chapter which you intend to implement to make Shabbat happen better this week. Tell a friend or family member what you are planning, and then do it!

MORE FOOD FOR THOUGHT

Abraham J. Heschel, *The Sabbath, Its Meaning for Modern Man*

You cannot go wrong with Rabbi Heschel, one of the greatest modern sages of our people. This book will help you appreciate Shabbat and keep you from ever simply going through the motions. Fluent in five languages, Heschel's English is sublime, and the book is worth owning for the sheer pleasure of the reading. But it is far more valuable than that. Get it in whatever edition you might find.

Mark D. Shapiro, *Gates of Shabbat [Sha'arei Shabbat]: A Guide for Observing Shabbat*

A well-respected guide to Shabbat observance from a Reform Jewish perspective.

Ron Wolfson, *Shabbat: The Family Guide to Preparing for and Celebrating the Sabbath*

A soup-to-nuts Conservative Jewish guide to the table rituals associated with Shabbat, complete with Hebrew texts, translations, and transliteration of all the prayers. Pedagogically savvy and well worth owning. For people who want to know how to do it and do it right.

Ron Wolfson, *Seder lel Shabat [The Shabbat Seder]*

This is the table "bencher" for each person at the table, supplying all the prayers, transliterated, as well as in Hebrew. This coordinates with the previously listed book but eliminates all the explanations.

TAKE-OUT

Ahad Ha'am (Asher Ginsberg, 1856–1927) wrote, "More than the Jews have kept the Sabbath, the Sabbath has kept the Jews." Against the background of this chapter, what does this quotation mean?

CHAPTER TEN

LET'S HAVE A *MEATING*

Let's take a minute to talk about your friends, your family, and eating together.

Why do you enjoy having a meal with friends and family, even with strangers? It's not just the food. If you were eating the same food, but all alone, would that be the same as eating with friends and family? We both know the answer to that one!

Something good, even magical, happens when people share a meal. Even strangers open up to one another, sharing their lives in ways that would not have happened if they hadn't sat together to eat. When we share a meal, we bond together. It seems we were created to eat in the company of others. To paraphrase Genesis, it is not good that man—or woman—should eat alone.

If eating together is magical, let's talk about how the magic happens and how it helps us grow as the people of God.

Say Hello to the Havurah

In the first century, it was the Jews who invented a meeting model called a havurah. This was a small-group fellowship that met to eat and study, to pray and build each other up in Jewish life, all the while setting an example for others. The Essenes of the Qumran community at the Dead Sea (famous for those scrolls) had similar groups. The Essenes were purists looking to counter religious corruption they attributed to the establishment in Jerusalem. But back in Jerusalem and beyond, the rabbis had their own havurot meeting in cities and villages. In these groups they sought to set a lifestyle example for the less learned common people.[1] Fast-forward about 2,000 years.

Interest in the havurah (sometimes spelled *chavurah*) exploded in the countercultural 1960s and 1970s. Beginning near Boston with *Havurat Shalom*, educated young Jews began experimenting with havurot. These young folks were zealous for Jewish life but disconnected from the religious institutions of their parents' generation. It is no big stretch to see that young people today feel the same estrangement, while seeking new communal models.

Havurot Among Yeshua's People

Besides the Pharisees and Dead Sea Essenes, another group of Jews gathered in havurot, eating, studying, and praying together to grow in their life of faith. These were Yeshua's first-century followers, whose havurah model (which some today call house churches) spread beyond the first century, Israel, and the Jewish world. Most people do not realize that this kind of home meeting was the invariable norm among Yeshua-believers, both Jews and non-Jews, throughout the Roman Empire until the fourth century! Gathering in a home around a common table was natural for the family of God.

Let's look at why this worked and how we can make it work for us.

How the Magic Happens

The theme song of the 1980s TV sitcom *Cheers* had it right: "Sometimes you wanna go where everybody knows your name." Everybody needs face-to-face community where people drink or eat together. Socialization changes, stories flow, jokes get told, personal ties get stronger, and people leave strengthened by something more than food or drink.

A Yeshua-type havurah is a household meeting that is familial rather than formal, where people meet together, eat together, pray together, learn together, and grow together that they might go and better serve God's purposes in the world. In a Christian context, this is a house church, or home church.

Making Havurot Hum

Here's a select list of start-up concepts and practices for havurot. I call these The Eleven Fs.

1. Food

Good food is crucial whenever people get together. Eating together turns the ignition key for the social engine. Every viable havurah must include food at its gatherings, which Wolfgang Simson whimsically refers to as "meatings." This does not mean you need to eat a full meal together, although that's always nice. But it does mean something beyond potato chips, pretzels, and Coke! Generally, a potluck meal works well, but other noshes will do just as well.

2. Fun

Here, we do not mean silliness or games, but that people should enjoy being there. Otherwise, why should they come and why bother returning? The meetings should have good "vibes," and people should go away feeling their lives grew larger because they came. You'll want to identify gifted facilitators and hospitable hosts who like having people over, but who avoid being control-freaks! And yes, well-done music will certainly increase the enjoyment, if the nature of the particular havurah warrants it.

3. Faith

These meetings should get beyond having fun together. Our constant goal is to move our faith journey forward individually and together. "Faith" is not just inner ideas and convictions: it is all about how we live and why we choose the things we do. Yeshua told his followers to go into all the world and to teach people to *do* whatever he had commanded them. Faith is transformative; it leads to doing. Being a disciple is being an apprentice to the Master. As Yeshua said, "The student is not above the teacher, nor a servant above his master. It is enough for students to be like their teachers, and servants like their masters." (Matthew 10:24–25, NIV)

We'll want to see people leaving our havurah meetings motivated, inspired, and equipped for *tikkun olam*, repairing and healing our broken world and the people who share it with us. A good havurah grows our faith.

4. Folks

You can't have a havurah meeting without folks, but the folks you choose will determine what kinds of questions, discussions, and community you will have. Here's a hint: *People reproduce after their kind. The kinds of people you have will determine the kinds of people you get.* If you are especially seeking to serve Jewish and intermarried people and households, these are the kinds of people you should choose to "seed" your havurah. If you are especially seeking young people, you will need to seed your havurah with that age group. Just remember, "What you *seed* is what you get."

Some will find these kinds of considerations distasteful, and view selectivity in community formation to be unkind and exclusionary. Even unspiritual. But the research matters.

Priya Parker is the biracial, bicultural founder of Thrive Labs. In *The Art of Gathering: How We Meet and Why It Matters*, she delivers a healthy reality check about how to form our various groups and about the need to not only select carefully, but also to exclude carefully.

> The crux of excluding thoughtfully and intentionally is mustering the courage to…shift your perception so that you understand that people who aren't fulfilling the purpose of your gathering are detracting from it, even if they do nothing to detract from it. This is because once they are actually in your presence, you (and other considerate guests) will want to welcome and include them, which takes time and attention away from what (and who) you're actually there for. Particularly in smaller gatherings, every single person affects the dynamics of a group. Excluding well and purposefully is reframing who

and what you are being generous to—your guests and your purpose.[2]

The people you have in your havurah group will determine your focus, the issues that will be addressed, and the questions that will be asked and answered. Such group members will exercise this influence not only by what they say, but by who they are. The gravity of the meeting will naturally shift toward addressing the concerns of those making up the group. Therefore, in forming a havurah, keep your focus in mind, and recruit accordingly. As your group grows, what kinds of people do you want to attract, to serve? It is no sin to be particular about what kind of seed you sow when you are looking for a particular crop. Remember the wisdom of Priya Parker, and read her book—one of the fine resources out there to help us with our planning and community growth.

5. Formulas

Having a freewheeling "whatever happens happens" meeting philosophy is a deal-breaker. People are busy, and they don't come to meetings to "chill." People will instead come and return to purposeful meetings that address their felt needs and where meaningful things get done. Your havurah meetings will need to have a distinct character, a kind of fiber, what I call "crunch." People like crunchy meetings that give them something to chew on.

A good havurah will have a sense of purpose, and communicate its distinctive character through developing its own language, characteristic metaphors, and ways of thinking. Let's call these "formulas." It's a good idea to be intentional about communicating your purpose and the language you employ. Develop concepts and metaphors that members and visitors will associate with you, shaping their imaginations and understanding of what you stand for. This will motivate and equip them to share with others the nature of your group.

6. Finding the Right Location

Retailers say it's all about "location, location, location." That's true here, too. Things tend to break down when the site of a havurah is so remote that participants have trouble traveling to it or finding it. This problem is mitigated if you rotate from house to house in holding your meetings. But still, location matters. Make it easy, not hard, to get to your group. Make it easy, not hard, for your group to succeed.

7. Funding

Establishing havurot among Jewish people generally means doing so in cities. But here's the problem: Doing anything in cities gets expensive.

When planting spiritual projects among Jewish people and outreach projects among Jews, money and the lack of it often determine possibilities. Sometimes, the need to maintain cash flow shapes decision-making so that you choose to do what will "sell" to the donor base instead of pursuing other priorities. And always, you can only attempt what you can afford.

Havurah groups solve this problem because even in cities, costs are absurdly low. What is the chief expense for a havurah meeting? It's food! And that expense is covered by hosts/hostesses or is shared among group members so that it is as easy as a piece of cake, or a bagel with cream cheese and lox. These low costs leave a surplus of funds available for all sorts of projects and experiments, like guest speakers, guest musicians, and periodic larger gatherings.

8. Flocking

Havurot groups are the relational backbone that sustains growing Yeshua-believing communities. The flock grows through multiplying havurot, not through addition. For meetings of Yeshua believers, bigger is not better and small is beautiful. It is imperative that we set limits on how large a havurah will be, and provide for growth through planting new ones that will also set limits on their size, while planting new groups themselves. Generally, havurot should have between six and fifteen participating members. Any smaller than six, and introverts will feel too exposed to participate. Any larger than fifteen, and newcomers will have to fight to break in and be heard. Because havurah meetings are fundamentally participatory, these factors, the floor of six people and the ceiling of fifteen people, should be kept in mind. The size of the group will determine the quality of relationship and interaction.

There are many ways to serve the children in our groups. They may participate in the meeting, they may amuse themselves while the meeting progresses, members of the havurah may serve as teachers and caregivers to children during at least part of the meeting—the possibilities are as wide as your creativity and imagination. They vary with the nature of the group and the activities of the hour.

One thing is certain: Relationship is crucial. Yeshua discerned that the two greatest commandments are relational and interlocked: "'You are to love ADONAI your God with all your heart, with all your soul, with all your understanding and with all your strength.' The second is this: 'You are to love your neighbor as yourself'" (Mark 12:30–31, CJB). These commands cannot be separated, and both are relational. This is why we also read, "If anyone says, 'I love God,' and hates his brother, he is a liar. For if a person does not love his brother, whom he has seen, then he cannot love God, whom he has not seen" (1 John 4:20, CJB). We need face-to-face groups where all can grow in their love of God and each other. Havurah groups are familial groups where relationship happens. Such households are the fulcrum for moving the world in directions that please God.

Too often, other less-relational structures prevail. How many of us have visited a house of worship, perhaps multiple times, without anyone asking our name, and without even learning the names of those with whom we gathered? Larger gatherings preclude that level of intimacy. This is not the dynamic that changed the world in three centuries, and it is not the kind of relational culture that kept the Jews a people in a two-millennia diaspora.

A bigger-is-better philosophy breeds spectator spirituality. When your meeting place is dominated by a platform that is really a stage, with a worship team that is a band, and a clergy person who is an inspirational speaker, what you are calling a congregation is really an audience. No matter how good and how entertaining the event, and how earnest the spiritual preparation, the context and the structure of the gathering is neither transformational nor relational. People are not truly known, their needs are not expressed, and their gifts are not developed. In such an environment where hardly anybody knows your name, members of the family of God may just remain strangers.

Nothing we have said here should ever be understood to exclude larger meetings from our plans. Such meetings also serve necessary purposes, supplementing but never replacing the more foundational and relational havurah meetings.

These necessary and supplemental larger meetings are called Five Cs Meetings.

9. Five Cs Meetings

Like havurot or home-churches, Five Cs meetings are based on a biblical model. When both models work in tandem, performing their own proper functions, they constitute the "bones," the infrastructure of the community.

These two kinds of meetings sustained and grew the Yeshua Movement among first-century Jews. Two references in Acts highlight these two models:

> And day by day, *attending the temple together and breaking bread in their homes*, they received their food with glad and generous hearts, praising God and having favor with all the people. And the Lord added to their number day by day those who were being saved.... And not for a single day, *either in the Temple court or in private homes*, did they stop teaching and proclaiming the Good News that Yeshua is the Messiah.
> (Acts 2:46–47 ESV; Acts 5:42, CJB; italics mine)

The home meetings were the forerunners of our havurah meetings. Of course, since the time of the Babylonian Captivity in the sixth century BCE, Jews had synagogues, places of prayer, communal gathering, and instruction. Priests and Levites gathered there for prayer at the same times of day that other priests and Levites were serving in the Jerusalem Temple. Other Jews would join with them in prayer. As the synagogue as an institution, it increasingly resembled the Temple in the purposes it served, which we term "the Five Cs."

Connection—Linkage to a wider tradition and community across time. This includes rites of passage, rituals, Holy Days, etc.

Celebration—Of God and His mighty acts.

Catalysis—Energizing and focusing participants to commit to and serve core community values and purposes.

Communal Prayer—Gathering together to seek God's face.

Children—A context where the next generation will see that the spirituality of their home has a wider communal context.

Five Cs meetings are just as important today as they were in the first century. Assume that you are involved in a local network of four havurot, with a total of 35 adults and 14 children. The foundational meeting for face-to-face spirituality is the havurah meeting. But what would it be like if these groups met together once a week, or once every two weeks, or once a month, for a Five Cs meeting, with all havurah participants in attendance? Such meetings would include a Torah service, weddings, B'nai Mitzvah, liturgical, calendrical, and ritual events of all kinds, etc.

Let's not forget the issue of expenses in urban areas. Urban congregations who own or rent a building for their use seven days a week, or even once or twice every week, incur considerable expenses. But what if we held such meetings less frequently in rented facilities? And what if some of these larger meetings were online as well in one location? Expenses would fall dramatically.

Until now, the default model for Messianic Jews has been to share a facility with a church, with weekly or even daily access, often with office space included. In some cases, Messianic congregations own their own facilities. But both of these approaches are expensive. Wouldn't it be a good idea to explore other less expensive options that leave us with greater liquidity for special events, projects of various kinds, and philanthropy?

One promising variation would be to have a hub center to service all the havurot in a larger metropolitan area. This would be the place for Five Cs meetings, also providing enhanced educational and media possibilities. Ideally, there would be a considerable number of havurot members there whose contributions would support the center. Support might also be supplemented by philanthropy.

If this hub were open for business 24/7, I fear it would be simply a variation on a prevailing model and would risk subordinating proper spiritual priorities to financial needs. This must not be allowed to happen. The lure of bigger is better is a severe temptation, so I favor periodically contracted rental space for Five Cs meetings, as previously discussed. However, perhaps I lack imagination. That remains to be seen. But it is imperative that our communal structures remain mission-driven rather than budget-driven. Other variations on the Havurah/Five Cs complementary model remain to be discovered, devised, and discussed.

And for those of you who are iffy about exploring new models, consider this: Could it not be that with changing times, we ought to reconsider our default assumptions? That was certainly the case during the countercultural revolution of the late 1960s and early 1970s that gave rise to the modern havurah movement and the Jesus Revolution. And couldn't that money that we have been spending on buildings and rent be better invested in events featuring outside talent, on paying professionals that serve our needs, educational programs, philanthropy, and humanitarian aid projects?

Whatever future we imagine, if our communities are to have the kind of bones that sustained the Body of Messiah in the first three centuries and turned the Roman world upside down, we must have foundational and relational havurah meetings, that is, havurot in the Jewish world and home-churches in the Christian context, complemented by periodic Five Cs meetings.

10. Fuel

Sustained engagement with Scripture and with the Divine Presence—the *Ruach HaKodesh*—is the irreplaceable fuel of a dynamic havurah.

Immersion in Scripture and sound teaching is always foundational, while the Divine Presence is the always-active senior partner in all that we do. Beyond being a doctrine to believe in, we may learn by experience to perceive the Presence of the Spirit, sometimes as an added joy, sense of unity, or an added wisdom that surfaces in individuals or within the group. Various spiritual gifts will manifest among us as well. This perceived reality of the *Ruach* will be subtle, somewhat fragile, but real. The *Ruach* illumines our path and empowers our community. Saul of Tarsus, aka the Apostle Paul, put it this way: "I planted, Apollos [one of his associates] watered, but God gave the increase" (1 Cor 3:6, ASV). It is always God who does the heavy lifting.

11. Five Foundational Functions

We have already looked at the bones of the community viewed as the Body of Messiah, the infrastructure of the kinds of gatherings that sustain our common life. But what of the organs and systems of that Body? Scripture reminds us there are five functions or systems that sustain the life of the Body when they are working together in harmony.[3]

Many people interpret these five functions as offices and titles for people to bear. But that kind of hierarchy can get stultifying and self-aggrandizing. It's far better to simply think of these as functions or organic systems of our communal body-life. These are analogous to biological systems such as the endocrine, circulatory, digestive, skeletal, and lymphatic systems.

Paul speaks of these functions as gifts distributed by the ascended Messiah especially for the growth of his people. And (no surprise) he links these gifts to the metaphor of a body, as we do. Writing to the Ephesians, he names these five functions as **the emissaries, the prophets, the evangelists, the pastors (shepherds), and teachers**.

These labels are rather grandiose. Many of us recoil from them. Perhaps it's because they sound so religious. Perhaps it's because we associate them with heavy-handed control, religious showboating, or authoritarian abuses. All of these are good reasons. It is right to be leery. But Paul's model is not threatening but life-giving. Notice how warmly he outlines the purposes of these functions as they work in harmony with each other:

> Their task is to equip God's people for the
> work of service that builds the body of the
> Messiah, until we all arrive at the unity
> implied by trusting and knowing the Son

of God, at full manhood, at the standard
of maturity set by the Messiah's perfection.

We will then no longer be infants tossed
about by the waves and blown along by
every wind of teaching, at the mercy of
people clever in devising ways to deceive.
Instead, speaking the truth in love, we will
in every respect grow up into him who is
the head, the Messiah. Under his control,
the whole body is being fitted and held together by the support of every joint, with
each part working to fulfill its function;
this is how the body grows and builds
itself up in love. (Eph 4:12–16, CJB)

This is nurturing language. It is comforting and
reassuring. The Life-giver is the Presence of God who
equips and calls various members of the community to
perform these functions as he sees fit.

Let's look at these not as offices and titles, but as
five functions.

Some of these gifted people perform *the emissary
function* (Alan Hirsch calls them "envoys"). Writing to
the Corinthians, Paul terms these emissaries "master
builders/architects" with overall oversight and a vision
for what the community is about. People performing

the emissary function embody a God-given vision of where the community should be heading. In a sense, they incarnate the future and call people to make it happen.

The prophet function is also scary, an often-misunderstood term. In the Newer Testament sense, it flows through people with highly developed intuitive gifts whose sensitivity to the *Ruach* enables them to "read" the current situation, to sense "what's in the air," and to provide key insights to help guide and warn the community. Prophets call the community back to commitments they never should abandon, always watching over the community's well-being. The Prophet Hosea describes such a person as "a man of the spirit, or a watchman" (Hosea 9:7–8, CJB).

The evangelistic function is performed by people especially gifted to win a hearing for the Good News of Yeshua, people whom others trust and admire, and to whom they will listen. I term these people "gospel magnets" who attract people to the Good News, who engage others through their outgoing and receptive manner, and who communicate the Good News of Yeshua in a way that clicks with the particular people with whom they are in conversation. These are good communicators and gifted metaphor-makers.

Pastoring or shepherding means being especially attentive to the well-being of the members of the community. People gifted for this role are the first to notice when someone is absent, troubled, or neglected. They have an eye and a heart for people, always concerned with the safety and nurture of the flock.

Teachers present relevant spiritual truth in a structured, logical, dependable, and retainable manner.

These five kinds of functions, which we term "Body-systems," lead people to maturity and effectiveness in serving God. Members of any spiritual community should pray that God would raise up such functions within the Body. When these functions are present in a balanced and abundant manner, all heaven breaks loose!

Just an extra word, also based on the example of Scripture: Just as our physical systems need to be checked and monitored by physicians, so these spiritual systems, and the Bodies in which they are functioning, remain healthy through periodic checkups and attention. Havurah communities need outside consultants and advisors who function like physicians. These physicians and consultants, what some term "apostolic teams," keep an eye out for the health of the community and will check in with them to determine if all of these functions are present and in balance.

Alan Hirsch reminds us that these five functions describe who Yeshua was when he lived among us. In a sense, then, when operating well, these functions help our communities to embody and reflect Yeshua's character, extending His presence in the world.

FOR BETTER DIGESTION

1. Would you say that participating in small groups (under fifteen people) has played a dynamic role in your spiritual development?

2. Of the eleven featured concepts and practices for havurot, can you name three that particularly stand out as non-negotiables? Which ones? Why?

3. Have you ever participated in a worshipping community where you realize you didn't know most of the people nor they, you?

4. Do you agree or disagree that relationship with people and relationship with God are coordinate, so that poor ways of relating to either people or to God contaminates both spheres? Why is that?

MORE FOOD FOR THOUGHT

On the Havurah

Bernard Reisman, *The Chavurah: A Contemporary Jewish Experience*

One of the earliest treatments of the phenomenon providing solid historical background as well as early assessments of the havurah movement in the 1970s. Essential.

Riv-Ellen Prell, *Prayer & Community: The Havurah in American Judaism*

A thorough study of the 1970s countercultural havurah from a participant observer anthropologist. Excellent and essential.

Ron Wolfson, *Relational Judaism: Using the Power of Relationships to Transform the Jewish Community*

A necessary corrective to doctrinaire institutionalism, calling for a more relational approach to community formation. Another essential book.

The National Havurah Committee website: https://havurah.org/

Surprisingly sparse website which seems to betoken a loss of dynamism for the 1970s era havurah.

On the Home-Church/House-Church

Robert J. Banks and Julia Banks, *The Church Comes Home*

The book describes and promotes the founding of home churches and home-church-based congregations (two related but different entities), and defines the former as "a kind of extended Christian family that involves singles, intermarrieds, and their children. It meets regularly to communally develop a shared Christian life, to relate each member's faith to everyday life, and to deepen each member's relationship with

God. They may meet in a house, a condominium, or an apartment—wherever 'home' is for members of the group and wherever they feel most 'at home.' Features interviews with people experimenting with variations in the model. A great book. Don't miss this one.

Robert J. Banks, *Paul's Idea of Community: The Early House Churches in Their Cultural Setting*

Another essential book providing a historically rooted argument for, and description of, house churches. Rob Banks is not only a scholar but also was a leader in the house church movement for a decade—a world-class expert with whom I studied with great benefit.

TAKE-OUT

Remember! Small is beautiful.

CHAPTER ELEVEN

CALENDAR IN THE KITCHEN: A FAMILY AFFAIR

Rich takes his girlfriend Shari out for dinner. It's her birthday. Looking into her expectant, beaming eyes, he says: "Forget about the past, you can't change it. Forget about the future, you can't predict it. Forget about the present, I forgot to get you one."

Is this guy in trouble?

Did you ever forget a loved one's birthday? Your significant other? Your spouse? Your parent? A family member? Was this cool with all concerned or was it a real no-no? I would guess the latter.

Why the big deal? Simple. When we remember someone's significant dates, we show how significant they are to us. But when we forget, whether we intend to or not, we telegraph disregard.

It's the same with our relationship with God and our fellow Jews worldwide throughout time. Not remembering important dates, not marking them in a special way, may indicate a weak relationship, irresponsibility, and disregard. Ouch.

Many of us grew up in homes that had a calendar hanging in the kitchen. Despite being quite digital, thank you, my wife and I have one of these in our kitchen even now. On calendars like ours, you'll find dates circled and maybe a scribbled note: Abby's birthday. Judy's anniversary. Dad's *yahrzeit* (memorial of day of passing from this life). The circles and notes on the calendar are evidence of love, of relationship, and of bonds that should never be broken.

The Jewish family across time has such a calendar. When we pay attention to it, we show that we regard other Jews as family, and that being part of this people means something to us. We also show respect for God, our Father, remembering him, what he asks of us, and how much we owe him. In addition to remembering the dates, we will often eat special foods, or perform rituals related to those dates. Whether we intend to or not, letting those dates slip by unnoticed and not honored can and often does signify a loosening of our bonds with our people and our God.

This is not the place to give an in-depth study of the holy days and memorial occasions marked on the Jewish calendar. But because this custom—honoring such days—is so crucial to family awareness and solidarity, I offer you the following chart to give you a bare sketch of the most prominent of these special Jewish occasions, and when they occur. I also sketch their purpose or what they commemorate, including the gatherings, foods, and rituals attached to each occasion. And here's a reminder. For most of these, you can find greeting cards. Send them. Even if it's digital.

The purpose of this chart? To inform, to remind, and to awaken. All of us can improve our act by learning from this chart. I leave out Shabbat because we already devoted a full chapter to that one. But see below for others, although again, this list is not fully comprehensive. And remember, this is only a sketch. There is always more to know and to do. But let's begin.[1]

Rosh HaShanah

Time of Year
August-September

Purpose, Commemoration
Commemorates the Creation; Marks the beginning of Ten Days of Awe, a time of reflection and repentance with a focus on accountability to God.
Traditionally, these ten days are when we assess the lessons of the past year and seek God's wisdom for how to make the next year better than the last.

Gatherings
Services at a local synagogue on the night before the 1st day of Rosh HaShana, extensive services all day on the 1st and, for the more observant, also the 2nd day of Rosh HaShanah.

Actions
Hear the sound of the shofar at synagogue.

Tashlich during the ten days, a ceremony at a flowing body of water where we throw crumbs, symbolizing our sins, into the water as a metaphor for God's separating us from our sins, which are now irretrievable in the depths of the sea.

Foods
Apples dipped in honey—a harbinger for a sweet year to come.

Round loaves of challah bread, symbolizing the returning cycle of the year.

Yom Kippur

Time of Year
August-September

Purpose, Commemoration
Day of solemn repentance at the end of the Ten Days of Awe as an appeal to God for a good year to come.

Gatherings
Services at a local synagogue the night before and all day on Yom Kippur.

Special added prayer (*Yizkor*) on Yom Kippur in remembrance of departed loved ones.

Actions
Abstain from food, water, and sexual relations.

Foods
A day of fasting!

Sukkot

Time of Year
September/ October

Purpose, Commemoration
Celebration of the harvest; memorial of God's providing for us during the 40 years of wilderness wandering.

Gatherings
Special synagogue services.

Waving a *lulav* (set of branches of four trees) and an *etrog* (relative of the lemon) in a special manner is an ancient appeal for water and agricultural sustenance.

Actions
Building a *sukkah*.

Whenever possible, eat meals in the sukkah, and even sleep there!

Foods
Agricultural produce.

Simchat Torah

Time of Year
September/ October

Purpose, Commemoration
Celebrates the gift of Torah at Mt. Sinai and marks our having read through the entire Torah in the prior year and beginning to read it again!

Gatherings
Go to synagogue for a time of festive dancing celebrating the gift of Torah.

Actions
Dancing with the Torah at the synagogue.

Children march with flags as if they are soldiers of Torah.

Foods
No special foods.

Hanukkah

Time of Year
December

Purpose, Commemoration
Celebrates the capture and rededication of the Jerusalem Temple in 164 BCE.

Gatherings
Rituals are generally done at home.

Actions
The lighting of candles in a *hanukkiah* (a nine-branched *menorah* especially for this occasion). A *hanukkiah* has eight branches for each of the eight days of the festival, and the ninth branch to hold the candle used to light all the others.

Children play with a special top called a *dreidl* in a gambling game, usually for chocolate coins or other goodies; all sing Hanukkah songs.

Foods
Foods fried in oil, especially potato pancakes (*latkes*) and also *sufganiyot* (jelly doughnuts).

Tu B'Shevat

Time of Year
January/February

Purpose, Commemoration
The New Year for Trees. Torah law in the Land of Israel indicated that trees had to be at least four years old before offerings could be made from their fruit. Then the following year and thereafter, the fruit was available for common use. Therefore, this date is the annual birthday for trees—a reference point for computing the age of a fruit tree.

Gatherings
None.

Actions
Often environmental and ecological themes and events will be explored at this time. It is also a time for planting trees either here or in Israel.

Foods
Fruits and nuts that grow on trees.

Purim

Time of Year

Late February, March

Purpose, Commemoration

Celebrates the rescue of the Jewish people from a planned genocide in Persia; a celebration of victory over foes who are viewed as buffoons.

Gatherings

Gathering in the synagogue for the reading of the entire Book of Esther, often presented as a dramatic, musical, comical event in plays called "Purim *Shpiels*."

Everyone comes in costume, often as characters in the story of Esther—the funnier and more ridiculous, the better.

Actions

It is traditional to give money to charity and send anonymous packages of goodies to your friends and family.

In some communities it is allowed to get more than a little tipsy. This holiday is a safety valve expressing Jewish relief over not always being the victim.

Foods

Three-cornered pastries called *Oznei Haman* (Haman's ears) or *Hamentaschen*. Some eat other foods with something hidden inside.

Pesach (Passover)

Time of Year

Late March or April

Purpose, Commemoration

Celebrates our redemption from Egypt.

Gatherings

Gathering at home.

Actions

Gather at home for a *seder*, a festive meal including readings from the *Hagaddah*, the story of our redemption from Egypt, and poems, songs, and legends commenting on the same.

Some Jews hold *seders* on the first and second day of Passover; others do it only the first day.

Foods

For the eight days of the Passover season, religious Jews avoid leavened grain products, and instead of eating bread, eat matzah.

Other foods to be eaten include matzah ball soup, gefilte fish, macaroons, cookies and cakes made without yeast but with nuts (although some Jewish traditions forbid nuts at Passover).

Shavuot

Time of Year

Fifty days after the first day of Passover

Purpose, Commemoration

Commemorates the first fruits of the harvest, which were brought to the Temple as an offering. An alternative name for Shavuot is *Hag ha-Bikkurim* (the Festival of the First Fruits). It also commemorates the giving of the Torah at Mount Sinai, so it is also termed *Hag Matan Torateinu* (the Festival of the Giving of Our Torah).

This was also the time when the Spirit was poured on Yeshua's people. In the Church calendar it is called Pentecost.

It is celebrated for one or two days, depending on community custom.

Gatherings

Special services are held at synagogue. This is also a day when religious Jews do not go to their jobs and regular activities.

277

Actions

In celebration of the gift of Torah, on the first night of Shavuot, religious Jews gather to study together until dawn, followed by a *shacharit* service. The event, known as *Tikkun Leil Shavuot*, often involves special teachers, lectures, and prepared lessons.

Foods

It is customary to eat dairy foods at this time, and cheesecake is a big favorite!

Yom HaShoah

Time of Year

Europeans celebrate it on the anniversary of the liberation of Auschwitz, January 27.

The Israeli government links it to the Warsaw Ghetto Uprising, 27 Nisan, which remains the date most commonly observed by Jews.

Purpose, Commemoration

Memorializes the death of the six million in the Nazi genocide.

Gatherings

As a new observance, there are no established traditions, but Jewish community centers, synagogues, and institutions often sponsor related memorial and educational events and lectures.

Actions

It is appropriate to demonstrate solidarity with our people and to attend community events that may be held in your area.

Congregations and gatherings of Jewish Yeshua-believers should teach about Jewish survival, the threat of anti-Semitism, and mourn over the *Shoah* (Holocaust) at this time.

Foods
No special foods, and fasting is not mandated.

Yom HaZikaron

Time of Year

Fourth day of Iyar, the day before Yom HaAtzma'ut, in April or May

Purpose, Commemoration

This is Israel's somber Memorial Day, a national day of public mourning, memorializing those who gave their lives in defense of the State of Israel.

Gatherings

All places of entertainment are closed, and two-minute sirens are sounded throughout all of Israel, one in the evening to mark the beginning of the holiday and one in the morning, prior to the nation's public memorial ceremony at Mt. Herzl.

Outside of Israel, Yom Hazikaron is commemorated together with Yom HaAzmaut. There is usually a short memorial or a moment of silence preceding the communal Yom Ha'atzmaut celebration.

Some congregations add a special reading, often just before preceding the recitation of the Mourner's Kaddish.

Actions

In Israel, radio and TV programming highlight the great price paid in human lives for the founding of the Jewish state, retelling the story, speaking of fallen heroes.

In the Diaspora, the day and the sacrifices attached to it should be memorialized in a communal manner.

Foods

No special eating regulations.

Yom HaAtzma'ut

Time of Year
Fifth day of Iyar, in April or May

Purpose, Commemoration
Celebrates the founding of the Modern State of Israel.

Gatherings
Often fairs and big events celebrate the founding of the State of Israel.

Actions
Attend one of the fairs or celebratory events, and bring a friend!

Foods
Some people take this opportunity to eat Israeli foods.

Lag BaOmer

Time of Year

33 days after Passover, in May or June

Purpose, Commemoration

Lag BaOmer falls during the seven weeks between Passover and Shavuot. During that time, there is a custom of "counting the *Omer*" meaning counting the 49 days between the second day of Passover and Shavuot. An *omer* is an ancient Hebrew measure of grain, amounting to about 3.6 liters. Biblical law forbade any use of the new barley crop until after an *omer* was brought as an offering to the Temple in Jerusalem, which would be done on Shavuot.

Lag BaOmer is a shorthand way of saying "the 33rd day of the *Omer*."

Gatherings

Traditionally, Jewish weddings are not performed during the 50 days between Passover and Shavuot, except for this date, the 33rd day of counting the *Omer*, Lag Ba'Omer. So Jewish weddings are often held on this day, and children the age of three receive their first haircut on this day—a custom linked to how first fruits of trees were not to be offered until after three years.[2]

Actions

Traditionally Lag Ba'Omer is the day that Shimon Bar Yochai, a major Jewish mystic, died, but not before sharing with the world his mystical treatise, the *Zohar*. In celebration of that spiritual light, Jews traditionally have barbecues and bonfires on the evening when Lag Ba'Omer begins. Also, because Bar Yochai was reported to be sustained in a cave through a miraculous carob tree, it is customary to eat carobs at this time. This is also a day to practice conspicuous kindness, because Lag Ba'Omer is said to be the day when a plague was lifted that had killed 24,000 of Rabbi Akiva's disciples because of their failure to respect each other. There are other traditional activities as well.

Foods

There are not many traditional Lag B'Omer foods, but in Israel, typical foods eaten on the holiday include kebabs, pitas, eggplant salad, potato salad, tahini, etc. Otherwise, choose any foods that would go well at a picnic or bonfire.

Yom Yerushalayim

Time of Year

28th of Iyar, usually in May.

Purpose, Commemoration

Commemorates the reunification of Jerusalem under Israeli control after the Six-Day War. This was the first time Jews controlled the whole of Jerusalem since the Destruction of the Second Temple by the Romans in 70 CE.

Gatherings

In Jerusalem this is BIG day with many thousands of Jews filling the city. There will be dancing in the streets, and the plaza before the Western Wall is completely packed.

This reminds me of Ezekiel 36:38, where ADONAI promised, "like flocks of sheep for sacrifices, like the flocks of sheep in Yerushalayim at its designated times, in this degree will the ruined cities be filled with flocks of people. Then they will know that I am ADONAI."

Actions

In Jerusalem, special concerts and speeches are offered to celebrate the liberation of Jerusalem, which religious Zionist Orthodox Jews view to be a more significant miracle than the founding of the modern Jewish state.

In the Diaspora, some communities conduct special programs about Jerusalem, with scholarly addresses and festive celebrations.

Foods

No special foods.

Tisha B'Av

Time of Year

Ninth day of the month of Av, in July or August

Purpose, Commemoration

Commemorates the destruction of both Temples, and the resultant calamities. Other communal disasters linked to this date include the decree in 1492 to expel the Jews from Spain. World War I began on Tisha B'Av, setting in motion a chain of events leading to the *Shoah*/Holocaust.

There are many others besides.

Gatherings

Special synagogue services are held in which the Book of Lamentations is read (often chanted) with all participants sitting on the floor in darkness as a sign of mourning.

Actions

This is an important time for connecting with being part of a people who endured at great cost and amid much suffering.

It is right for us to make time for attending the special services held at this time.

Foods
This is a day of fasting.

FOR BETTER DIGESTION

1. If you use a digital or paper calendar that does NOT have these calendar events marked, go through it and mark the days so you don't miss them. And remember, Jewish holidays begin at sunset the night before.

2. Go online and discover one or more sites where you can send appropriate greetings cards for Jewish holidays. Mark that address on your digital devices.

3. On our chart, pick one Jewish holiday you have not normally observed, and make plans with at least one friend to observe it in some way this year.

4. Can you think of a time when someone surprised you by remembering some special event or date in your life? How did it make you feel, and why?

5. How might our patterns of observance be affected by thinking of God as a Father who asks us to remember these occasions?

MORE FOOD FOR THOUGHT

Abraham P. Bloch, *The Biblical and Historical Background of the Jewish Holy Days*

A thorough and well-organized survey of everything you wanted to know about the Jewish Holy Days. The best book available on the subject for those seeking usable and authoritative information.

Abraham P. Bloch, *The Biblical and Historical Background of Jewish Customs and Ceremonies*

A perfect companion to his work on the Jewish Holy Days, this volume explains the world of Jewish customs and ceremonies authoritatively and clearly. I wouldn't do without this book.

Darrell L. Bock and Mitch Glaser, *Messiah in the Passover*

A collection of accessible and scholarly articles providing a wealth of information for those seeking to view Jesus and the Last Supper through Jewish eyes. Very useful.

Mitch Glaser and Zhava Glaser, *The Fall Feasts of Israel*

Explains the fall feasts of Israel from a solid biblical base while giving readers an understanding of the importance and observance of these feasts in Jewish life.

Irving Greenberg, *The Jewish Way: Living the Holidays*

A good book by a humane and deeply respected Modern Orthodox Jewish leader. Helps you get beyond the machinery of observance into its soul. Good book. Great man.

Barney Kasdan, *God's Appointed Times: A Practical Guide to Understanding and Celebrating the Biblical Holy Days*

This is a good introduction for Christians who seek a foundation for understanding and celebrating the biblical holy days. Barney is a Messianic Jewish rabbi and writes in an easily accessible manner.

Sam Nadler, *Messiah in the Feasts of Israel*

I have known Sam Nadler for 50 years and more. He is a gifted teacher and writes from within a strongly conservative theological framework. Yeshua-believers who love the Bible will love this book.

Michael Strassfeld, Betsy Platkin Teutsch, and Arnold M. Eisen, *The Jewish Holidays: A Guide and Commentary*

A thorough and authoritative survey of the Jewish holidays. Well-written and comprehensive.

TAKE-OUT

We demonstrate respect for God when we remember the dates he asks us to remember. Likewise, disregarding these dates demonstrates a lack of respect for God and his people.

CHAPTER TWELVE

COOKIES ON THE TOP SHELF: MORE ON THE HENDRICKS METHOD

As we promised back in Chapter Two, this chapter fills in more steps and details for implementing the Hendricks Method of Bible study. It's okay if you don't want to go into such depth. It's also okay if you just don't want to do it now, but reserve the right to do so when you have more of an appetite. In either case, this material is here as a service to you if and when you want to stretch yourself to reach for these "cookies on the top shelf."

Taking the Hendricks Method to the Top Shelf

Let's pick up where we left off our discussion of the Hendricks Method from Chapter Two, beginning here with Step Five (of ten).

Step Five: Interpret what that evidence meant to its original author and audience.

Interpret by seeking to imagine and reconstruct how the text was understood by its human author and first hearers.

People often misinterpret the Bible because the only questions they bring to it are, "What do I get from this?" or, "What does this mean to me?" These are good questions, but they are always wrong when they are asked too early. They should only be asked and answered after rigorous examination has clarified the intended meaning of the author and its reasonable interpretation by his earliest hearers. Questions about what we get out of the passage are premature unless we can first give a good answer to this prior question: "As best I can determine, what did this text mean to its original hearers/readers and what was its author trying to say to them and to accomplish in the writing?" This is Ground Zero for responsible interpretation.

We need to prevent ourselves from drawing pleasing conclusions that have nothing to do with what the authors or God sought to convey. When interpreting the Bible, we need to get out of our own echo chamber or the echo chamber of our culture. We want to avoid always repeating the same ideas and themes, thinking these are true because they are so familiar.

We observe in order to see what the Bible says and how it says it; we *interpret* in order to clarify what the Bible is getting at by what it says. Fortunately, if you've been wearing your detective's hat and made accurate observations about the evidence (the text itself), you have already laid a solid groundwork for understanding what all of this is supposed to mean. Think of Sherlock Holmes, Adrian Monk, or Lieutenant Columbo.

What made them fascinating and effective? It was their extraordinary ability to observe. Great observations led to right conclusions. And in reading the Bible, the better your observations, the better your conclusions. We just have to discipline ourselves to do the grunt work and not jump to conclusions (interpretations) before all the evidence is in.

But how can we build a bridge between our observations and our conclusions? How do we reach our verdict about the meaning of the evidence?

Just pay attention to three factors that will build a bridge between observations and meaning.

1. **Content**—This is what you did in your observations. Kudos! You have sifted through the details of the text. Through noting comparisons, contrasts, metaphors, genres, repetitions, and emphases, you are now able to assess which textual evidence is more important, which is less so, and what all of this is supposed to mean.

2. **Repeated reading**—With repeated readings, certain details become apparent that you would have otherwise missed. Making a habit of rereading the text is like revisiting a crime scene to trigger a better conclusion about "who done it"!

3. **Context**—This factor is crucial to prevent reading something into the text that is not there. Just do this:

a. Consider the circles of textual context—Whether you are interpreting the meaning of a word, a verse, or a series of verses, it is always important to keep the immediate context in mind, and then to widen that area of concern to include the rest of the chapter. Then, if you need to, widen your investigation to the book itself, to other writings by the same writer, and if necessary, to other biblical books of the same period. Make it a habit to mentally construct a series of ever-wider concentric circles. Doing that will always lead you toward a justifiable interpretation of what the text is meant to say.

b. Pay attention to situational context—Especially with the letters of the Newer Testament, we should always seek to determine the situation the letter is addressing. What was going on with the recipients at that time? What questions were they asking of the apostle? What questions was he asking of them or seeking to answer for them? Sometimes the Book of Acts will help us to fill in details of the situational context of Paul's letters, and the biblical letter you are reading will always include details to help you understand the situation the writer is addressing and the problems he is seeking to solve.

c. Cultural context—Pay attention to the cultural context of the passage. Sometimes this is all that keeps us from major blunders.

For example, in Ruth 3:4, Naomi, the mother-in-law of the widowed refugee Ruth encouraged her to go into the harvest field at night where she would find their kinsman, Boaz, sleeping. Then she says, "When he lies down, note the place where he is lying. Then go and uncover his feet and lie down. He will tell you what to do." Ruth obeys, and in verse 9 she tells Boaz, "I am your servant Ruth.... Spread the corner of your garment over me, since you are a guardian-redeemer of our family."

It's so easy to misinterpret this passage by imposing our own cultural assumptions. By those assumptions, Naomi suggested that Ruth crawl into bed with Boaz and have sex with him as a means of drawing him into a marriage. But this is utterly wrong, because it fails to take into account the culture of the people in the text! In their culture, for a man to extend the corner of his blanket to a woman in this fashion was to indicate his intention of taking marital responsibility for her, which was the special responsibility of "guardian-redeemers," that is, male kinsmen responsible to care for widowed members of the clan.

To confirm this corrective interpretation, we just need to look at Ezekiel 16, where God compares Israel to an abandoned and vulnerable female child. Then he says this:

> Later I passed by, and when I looked at
> you and saw that you were old enough for
> love, I spread the corner of my garment
> over you and covered your naked body.
> I gave you my solemn oath and entered

into a covenant with you, declares the
Sovereign LORD, and you became mine.
(Ezek 16:8, NIV)

What is happening there? God uses this metaphor
to describe his taking spousal responsibility for Israel
the way kinsman-redeemers did.

You can see now how knowledge of the host culture
of the text of Ruth, as further illuminated by Ezekiel,
opens up the text for a correct interpretation, just as a
hasty and culturally intrusive interpretation of the text
would take us far away from Boaz's field into a left field
of our own!

d. Authorial context—The writers of Scripture were
not secretaries taking dictation from God; they wrote
within the context of their own personalities and individuality. Paul was not Peter; Peter was not John; and
Isaiah, Moses, Matthew, and Mark are different people
as well. Whether in the Older Testament or the Newer,
remember who is writing and interpret what you read
within the context of the thought world of that particular author. Here's an example: Luke, who wrote the
Gospel of Luke and the Book of Acts, was a physician.
As you read about healings in these books, notice how
he observes things the way a doctor would! And realize he is an expert at observing matters of sickness and
healing.

e. Chronological and historical context—Each author writes at a particular time, so keep in mind both the

times in which he lived and what other prophets of God were saying at the same time. Especially in reading the Older Testament, but also with the Newer Testament, many find it helpful to read outside sources supplying historical context for Bible texts we are reading. Besides the text of Scripture, carefully selected outside sources can help fill in context and broaden understanding.

f. Testamental Context—In addition to paying attention to the author's identity and when he wrote, keep in mind where the particular biblical book fits in the sweep of biblical revelation. As time went on, people understood matters more and differently than their predecessors did, because they had the benefit of prior revelation and had a cumulative understanding of what God was up to. This is called the progress of revelation. Ask yourself, "What Bible books were already in place when this book was written? What evidence is there that a given author is writing his Bible book with another Bible book in mind? Therefore, against what background should the author's intended meaning be interpreted? And in the broadest sense, how is the idea in the text you are examining developed in this particular Testament (and therefore, broad time period)?" I admit this is a high-level consideration. Still, it is a good one, and the broader your knowledge of Scripture, the easier it will be to apply this strategy.

g. Broad biblical context—This is the widest circle of context. Using a concordance (an index of all the words in the Bible), it can be helpful to compare what the entire Bible says most broadly on the subject under investigation. But never put this cart before the interpretational horse. Context is king—that is, the immediate context of the text you are examining. The closer our investigations are to the immediate context of a biblical text, the more reliable will be our conclusions about meaning. Using a concordance will bring you to texts that are centuries away from the text you are reading. So often, the conclusions you might draw from a concordance search will lead you away from the intended meaning of your text's immediate context. Some people will quickly glue together two texts written a thousand years apart as if they are one seamless thought. No. It doesn't work that way.

Step Six: Double-check your understanding with at least two translations besides the one you normally use.

Now that you have done your own work on the text, go check your perceptions against other Bible translations beyond the one you commonly use. (Of course, working in the original languages Hebrew, Aramaic, and Greek, is always preferable, but not many of us are equipped for that).

You may be accustomed to a word-for-word translation matching the original language with the closest English equivalent. The New American Standard Translation (NASB) is a highly regarded word-for-word translation. If this is your go-to version, try sleuthing for deeper understanding in a thought-for-thought translation intended to capture the impact the text might have had on its original hearers. The New International Version (NIV) is good for this. Another is the English Standard Version (ESV). Both the NIV and ESV sound natural when read aloud, as does the New Living Translation. And of course, there are others.

I also suggest reading in one or two translations from a Jewish perspective. For the *Tanach* (the Older Testament), the Jewish Publication Society *Tanach* (JPS) is a helpful version for the Older Testament. A new translation of the Older Testament by Jewish scholar Robert Alter, *The Hebrew Bible: A Translation with Commentary*, has much to commend it for those who love scholarly detail. But it is pricey and long (3500 pages in a three-volume set)! For the Older and Newer Testaments, I recommend the always stimulating and useful Complete Jewish Bible (CJB), translated by David H. Stern. Another translation covering both Testaments from a Messianic Jewish perspective is the *Tree of Life* version.

Step Seven: Meditate on the text to sense its significance for your own life and situation.

Chances are when you think of meditation, you think of someone blissed out in lotus position. That's Eastern meditation and lots of people are doing that nowadays.

Biblical meditation is very different! Rather than emptying one's mind, here we focus the mind gently, persistently, and deeply on the basis of what we discover in God's text. In Deuteronomy 30:14, the Torah describes this in four phases: "But the word is very near you (phase one). It is in your mouth (phase two) and in your heart (phase three), so that you can do it (phase four)" (ESV). Let's take a closer look:

- *The word is very near us.* We encounter some holy idea, some text, in some way. Most often, it is through our reading and study of the Bible. Often, something in the text you have been studying seems to "have your name on it;" it "speaks to you." Such a text deserves your contemplation. So, you meditate on it by following the next steps.

- *The word is in our mouth.* In the Bible, meditation is mulling over the text, chewing on it, repeating it, and ruminating on it. We keep speaking it to ourselves, articulating it, and chewing on it in our words and thoughts.

- *The word is in our heart.* As we think about it, mulling over its meaning, perhaps intuiting some connections we didn't think of before, the weightiness of the text trickles down into our hearts—the command center of our being. It comes alive within us in some way.

- The desired end result is *that we can do it.* This word, this phrase begins to take root in our thought, emotions, speech, or action. A process like this inspires, instructs, and shapes how we live. The word is meant to shape our lives, and such a meditative process helps make that happen.

You will gain benefits from this practice that are better felt than "tell't." I encourage you to try it! It's a good way to slow down and let the lessons of the text link up with our interior life.

Step Eight: Tradition—Process all of this within the Jewish tradition and in consultation with the best insights of the Christian world.

We never really study alone, because in studying we never get away from who we ourselves are—members of a multigenerational community, and for Jews, MOTs, "Members of the Tribe." In fact, we are not meant to get away from who we are, as if that were truly possible. You may not be religious, you may even be antireligious, but if you are a Jew, you are part of a people with inborn privileges and obligations, a people who have always seen themselves accountable for a structured relationship with God, a people with a history to which we owe payback and a future for which we bear responsibility.

You can find a fascinating passage toward the end of Deuteronomy that nails this concept. Moses, who knows he is soon to die, is giving his final address to the people of Israel. And the people are preparing to cross over the Jordan into the Land of Promise under the leadership of Joshua. Look at this passage and count how many strata of Israel's society Moses mentions:

> Today you are standing, all of you, be-
> fore ADONAI your God—your heads, your
> tribes, your leaders and your officers—all
> the men of Isra'el, along with your little
> ones, your wives and your foreigners here
> with you in your camp, from the one who
> chops your wood to the one who draws
> your water. The purpose is that you should
> enter into the covenant of ADONAI your
> God and into his oath which ADONAI your
> God is making with you today, so that
> he can establish you today for himself as
> a people, and so that for you he will be
> God—as he said to you and as he swore to
> your ancestors, to Avraham, Yitz'chak and
> Ya'akov. But I am not making this covenant
> and this oath only with you. Rather, I am
> making it both with him who is standing
> here with us today before ADONAI our God
> and also with him who is not here with us
> today.
> (Deuteronomy 29:9–14[10–15], CJB)

Depending upon how you interpret the words, you will find from eight to ten strata of Israelite society named here. It's an overkill of explicitness. When the Torah does this, it is making a point. And what is the point? The point is to underscore how *everyone* of Israel was there that day when Moses led them in renewing their covenant relationship with God. And that is why it is so remarkable that Moses adds this: "But I am not making this covenant and this oath only with you. Rather, I am making it both with him who is standing here with us today before ADONAI our God and also with him who is not here with us today." So the big question is, "Who is that?" All the commentators, Jewish and Christian, agree: it is the future generations of Israel. That means Barbara Streisand was there. Stephen Spielberg, too. Your uncle Morrie and Aunt Rose. And you were there. So was I. Whether you are a Hasid living in Borough Park or an atheist Millennial in Williamsburg with JewBu parents, this is you.

And if you want to explore the niche of experiencing God as a central aspect of your life, you will need to come to terms with this: You are part of that people with whom Moses confirmed the covenant on the plains of Moab. That's why I can never forget what my son said to me, years ago: "Dad. Being assimilated is not eating a ham sandwich. It's forgetting who your people are." You can take that to the bank!

I hope like me, you dare to believe that God has been with the Jewish people through all our wanderings—geographical and spiritual. About 750 BCE, Isaiah said it this way: "In all their affliction He was afflicted, and the Angel of His Presence saved them; In

His love and in His pity He redeemed them; and He bore them and carried them all the days of old" (Isa 63:9, NKJV). God has continued to accompany us everywhere and through everything. And finding our way back from our spiritual wanderings to reconnect to our moorings includes remembering that by God's design, we are part of a people.

With this in mind, shouldn't we process our own insights into Scripture while interacting with how our people have thought of these things?

We won't always agree with what they have said, and we don't need to. Judaism forbids us to check our brains at the door. We aren't being called to simply acquiesce. Despite how we will differ with other Jews, in every way possible we should seek to keep the chain of communal discussion unbroken. There are only two choices: assimilation—forgetting who our people are, and integration, remembering that who we are is rooted in who God has called our people to be. Tevye the Milkman had a word for this: Tradition!

Some people are sure to think this is unacceptable because it cramps their style. It destroys their freedom to differ. That is an important objection, and if it's your objection, good for you! But this objection is based on a faulty assumption. Let me explain by telling a story.

In the twelfth century, there was a great Jewish scholar named Rabbi Shmuel ben Meir (1083–1174). He is known as the Rashbam, and he was the grandson of the famous Rashi. Like his grandfather, the Rashbam favored a straightforward and literalist interpretation of holy texts. He didn't like fanciful allegorical approaches. So, when he read the passage in the Torah about God's commanding Israel to "Tie them [God's commands]on your hand as a sign, put them at the front of a headband around your forehead" (Deut 6:8, CJB), Rashbam insisted that the passage was not talking about *tefillin*, literal boxes with Scripture in them that religious Jews tie on our hands and foreheads when we pray on weekday mornings. He insisted that this traditional understanding was wrong. He said the text was instead referring to our actions (on your hand) and thoughts (a headband) which should be guided by these commandments. I am sure most of us are inclined to agree with him here.

But then things get very interesting.

In another of his writings, the Rashbam goes to considerable lengths describing the proper way to make *tefillin*—those same leather boxes he thought were a misinterpretation of the text! What's going on here?

Rashbam's switch-hitting on this issue is an example of how Judaism honors both private (personal) truth and public truth. We are encouraged to think and to have our own opinions (private truth), but like Rashbam, when our opinions differ from the received way of doing things, we should not insist on our own way in a manner that tears the fabric of intergenerational continuity. It is more important to respect and preserve tradition, intergenerational communal continuity, than to demonstrate how smart we are by insisting that we are right and everyone else is wrong. But remember, despite this commitment to preserving the traditions, we are encouraged to think things through for ourselves and develop defensible convictions of our own!

So, let's respect the tradition that forms the basis of communal continuity. Let's interact with Jewish tradition as we make our way through life and through Scripture. Where we must differ, let us do so respectfully, and wherever possible, let's maintain the chain of traditional understandings and practice.

We who are Jewish believers in Yeshua should always remember that the God of Israel also called people from other nations to be members of his family. The same Spirit upon whom we depend dwells among them through the work of Yeshua. We Jews should always preserve and value our distinct character and calling. But it is also right that we compare our views with how Yeshua's people from among the nations have understood his word and his voice.

The Messianic Jewish think tank, Hashivenu, has a core principle that well expresses what I am saying here:

> Hashivenu affirms the titanic contributions and complementary relationship of the historical Church and the Synagogue to the ennoblement and advancement

of the human enterprise. We therefore encourage the Messianic Jewish community to avail itself of the insights of both institutions while critically evaluating the usefulness of such insights as we pursue maturation. We also recognize the tremendous value offered by contemporary cross-disciplinary scholarship.[1]

A final word on tradition. If it ain't broke, don't fix it. Don't throw out traditions just because they are old. Maintain communal continuity wherever you can!

Step Nine: Carefully apply the meaning of the text to your own situation.

Observation and interpretation consort together, giving birth to meaning. Once you have done your best to figure out what the text meant to its original writers and hearers, you are at last ready to ask the question, "What does this text mean for me? How does it apply to my life?" This is called *application*. Let's look at some guidelines.

1. Determine whether your passage is simply describing something that happened once upon a time, or if the text is teaching us something to believe or do now and in our own context. Sometimes we confuse a description with a recommendation or even a commandment. Although we can derive lessons from descriptive passages, we are on much more solid

ground applying passages to ourselves that we identify as written for our instruction and admonition, and that are therefore applicable to our situation. Therefore, see the next step.

2. Be sensitive to aspects of the text that are locked into a certain culture or a certain time. And also look for other texts that are easily transferrable to our current place and time. Don't apply what we learned about Ruth and Boaz to your own dating life! In other words, be attentive to what is "normative" and what is not. Always be asking, "How is my context and situation parallel to the biblical context in this passage?" and, "What lessons can I rightly transfer over and apply to my time and context from that faraway time and place?" Generally, the greater the parallels between your situation and that described in the Bible, the easier it will be to reliably apply the text to your own here-and-now. Also, remember that God may have worked in different ways at an earlier time than he is choosing to work today. Be open to that possibility and think about it as you draw lessons for your own life. This process demands a lot of us, but really, that's part of the fun!

3. You can be more certain that a directive or practice found in the Bible is normative for you, too, by considering the following questions.

a. Do you have reason to believe the text is rightly preserved (that this Bible passage is not a disputed text)?

b. After all the work you have done with this text, does its meaning seem clear to you now, or is it hung up somewhere?

c. Do others from your tradition and others who study the Bible agree that your perceived meaning is a valid one?

d. Is there a general consensus among scholars/ leaders concerning the circumstances to which this meaning/passage applies?

e. Are there other passages which contradict, modify, restrict, clarify, or limit your interpretation and application of this passage?

f. Does the Bible seem to indicate that this practice was for a particular time only, and that it is now outdated and no longer applicable?

g. Is the passage and its meaning validated or repeated elsewhere in the Bible or is this passage unique unto itself? (One needs to be especially careful whenever interpreting something that only occurs once in the Bible, because there are no checks and balances to see how it is used elsewhere. It is called a *hapax legomenon*, "a word or phrase that appears only once in a text, the works of an author, or the written record of a language."[2]

Learn to keep these things in mind, at least in the back of your mind. These are the kinds of questions we should always be asking ourselves. And always remember: In general, your certitude about applying a biblical passage or meaning to a contemporary situation will be greater to the degree that the biblical situation and yours are parallel in one or more ways.

Step Ten: Capture and communicate the impact of this text to share it for the benefit of others.

By now you have spent quite a bit of time on this passage. Now you have an opportunity to spread the wealth, helping others to benefit from what you have learned. Remember what Seneca, the wise Greek philosopher said: "When we teach, we learn."

You'll be doing yourself a favor if you will find a way to diagram, map out, or portray what you learned about and from the text you've been studying. This might include something like a Mind Map,[3] or a chart, or even just a simple pithy statement that epitomizes what you have come away with. Through the process of distilling your findings and communicating them to others, what you have learned will become yours for a lifetime. So, make things teachable and teach others. It remains the very best way for you to really learn and retain what you have been studying.

FOR BETTER DIGESTION

1. Have you ever encountered someone who opens the Bible at random, grabs a verse or two, and then takes it as a talisman for the day, without bothering with any

of Hendricks's steps? Do you think this is a reliable and sensible way to deal with the text?

2. Why might it be that the people who impress us with their spiritual weight and quality (gravitas) are most often people who have a deep relationship with Scripture?

3. We read in this chapter of learning from Jewish tradition. Some Yeshua believers think they have nothing to learn from Jewish tradition, thinking they can only learn spiritually from other Yeshua believers. What do you think of this opinion?

4. Studying Scripture is not simply an intellectual exercise. We must remember that God meets with us in our encounter with the text. In addition to interpreting what we read, often, we will experience the Spirit's nudge.

MORE FOOD FOR THOUGHT

(These additional references also appear at the end of Chapter Two. For complete publication information, please see the For Further Reading section.)

The Hendricks Method

https://www.biblestudymagazine.com/bible-study-magazine-blog/2016/7/27/howard-hendricks-4-bible-study-steps

David R. Bauer and Robert A. Traina, I*nductive Bible Study: A Comprehensive Guide to the Practice of Hermeneutics*

The most comprehensive treatment on Inductive Bible Study available. For those of you who like books that are the last word on a subject. Highly technical.

Howard G. Hendricks and William D. Hendricks, *Living by the Book*. Set of 2 books—book and workbook, paperback

User-friendly.

Robert A. Traina, *Methodical Bible Study*

The foundational book upon which inductive Bible study methods are based, such as the Hendricks method. Somewhat technical.

TAKE-OUT

Remember! Studying Scripture is not merely an intellectual exercise, but it should never be less that that. It's always a good idea to bring your "best game" to the study of Scripture.

AFTERWORD

WOULD YOU LIKE A GLASS OF HOT TEA?

It's been fun sharing these meals with you around the table. Before you go, let me offer you a hot drink. A glass of tea.

From my grandparents' generation I learned the virtue of serving guests hot tea in a glass. This custom goes back to Eastern Europe. And we would not use just any kind of glass. No. It would be a *yahrzeit* glass. Purchased at the supermarket, these glasses were filled with wax and a wick, forming a memorial candle to be burned on the anniversary of the death of a close relative. But after the candle burned out, one had a per-fectly good, hefty glass to be used from then on as the perfect vessel for a good, hot cup of tea.

To this day, if you go into a Jewish home and are served hot tea in such a glass, the glass will speak two messages to you. First, this is a home that honors Jew-ish tradition. This family would not have such glasses if they didn't burn such tradition-laden candles. And second, the glass would say you were being treated like family.

Suppose you visited another home where they served you hot tea in a cup with a skull and crossbones on it. What kind of message would this be sending? The first message would be, "Don't drink the tea!" The second message would be, "Regardless of the quality and temperature of the tea, this is not a warm welcome." My guess is you would leave that house as soon as possible. And I would be right behind you.

What does all of this have to do with you and me? As you might guess, we're not talking about tea but something else. These stories are a reminder that the vessels we use are as important as what we serve.

Here's the point. We should be sharing with others the living water of a relationship with Adonai mediated through Yeshua the Messiah. And whenever we do so, we must make sure that our means, our vessels of language and culture, communicate welcome and familiarity. *Yahrzeit* glasses are not cups with skulls and crossbones. We always want to come across as humble and affirming, especially when addressing Jewish people whose family history with Christendom is soaked in blood.

In everything we do, in all that we say, and in how we communicate our faith, our cultural vessels themselves must come across as *Jewish*-friendly.

We are sent into the world to serve the living water of Yeshua-faith, and to invite others to the Great God-Feast at the end of time. As we do, let's treat as precious both the living water itself as well as the cultural vessels of Jewish life and tradition. In all that we say and do, and in how we say and do it, let's offer our people the hospitality of the table God prepares for us all.

Shalom! And *L'chaim!*

ACKNOWLEDGMENTS

Everyone I have ever known has contributed to me being the person I am, and so all deserve thanks for the part they have played in making this book possible. But of course, I cannot name them and their contributions. To do so would take another book!

But I can and will thank those who have directly touched this project and helped make it happen. Unending thanks to Lisa Norman of Heart Ally Books, LLC for your wisdom, know-how, and encouragement. Thank you also, Lisa for being my web guru. Thanks, too, to your team member, Lori A. Brown, for your eagle eyes and fierce commitment to the Chicago Manual of Style. No detail can stand before you.

Linda Wolf of Network Publishing Partners walked me through a jungle of details and stylistic decisions, taking a very rough product and making it respectable enough to walk around in public. The task was long, and your patience longer. Thank you. Thanks as well to your crony and mine, Em Hurley of Teknigram Graphics, for the cover and art work in this book that will forever cause people to sit up and take notice.

Thanks, too, to Russ Resnik, not simply for writing the Foreword, but also for being such a constant friend, helping me make it through the long, dark night of bringing a book from idea to reality. Thank you, Russ.

Rabbi Jonathan Bernis, you and the people of Jewish Voice Ministries International have so generously helped provide financial support for me and my nonprofit, Interfaithfulness. By doing so you helped relieve me of much stress while providing psychological space for me to get my work done. Thank you, Jonathan. Your generosity will never be forgotten in this world or the next.

Finally, my thanks to my faithful companion in all aspects of life, my wife, Naomi. You are as wonderful as people say you are, and that is saying very much indeed.

Stuart Dauermann

APPENDIX

BIBLE ABBREVIATIONS

Abbreviations for the various versions of the Bible quoted (source: www.biblegateway.com)

ASV	American Standard Version
CJB	Complete Jewish Bible
ESV	English Standard Version
GNT	Good News Translation
KJV	King James Version
NABRE	New American Bible (Revised Edition)
NASB	New American Standard Bible
NET	New English Translation
NIV	New International Version
NKJV	New King James Version
NLT	New Living Translation
NRSV	New Revised Standard Version
RSV	Revised Standard Version
TLV	Tree of Life Version

Abbreviations for the books of the Bible and their Hebrew names

Older Testament

Abbreviation	Name	Hebrew Name
Gen	Genesis	B'resheet
Exod	Exodus	Sh'mot
Lev	Leviticus	Vayikra
Num	Numbers	B'midbar
Deut	Deuteronomy	D'varim
Josh	Joshua	Y'hoshua
Judg	Judges	Shof'tim
Ruth	Ruth	Rut
1 Sam	1 Samuel	Sh'mu'el Alef
2 Sam	2 Samuel	Sh'mu'el Bet
1 Kgs	1 Kings	M'lakhim Alef
2 Kgs	2 Kgs	M'lakhim Bet
1 Chr	1 Chronicles	Divrei-HaYamim Alef
2 Chr	2 Chronicles	Divrei-HaYamim Bet
Ezra	Ezra	Ezra
Neh	Nehemiah	Nechemyah
Esth	Esther	Ester
Job	Job	Iyov
Ps	Psalms	Tehillim
Prov	Proverbs	Mishlei
Eccl	Ecclesiastes	Kohelet
Song	Song of Songs/ Solomon	Shir-HaShirim
Isa	Isaiah	Yesha'yahu
Jer	Jeremiah	Yirmeyahu

Abbreviation	Name	Hebrew Name
Lam	Lamentations	Eikhah
Ezek	Ezekiel	Yechezk'el
Dan	Daniel	Dani'el
Hos	Hosea	Hoshea
Joel	Joel	Yo'el
Amos	Amos	'Amos
Obad	Obadiah	'Ovadyah
Jonah	Jonah	Yonah
Mic	Micah	Mikhah
Nah	Nahum	Nachum
Hab	Habakkuk	Havakuk
Zeph	Zephaniah	Tz'fanyah
Hag	Haggai	Hagai
Zech	Zechariah	Z'kharyah
Mal	Malachi	Mal'akhi

Newer Testament

Abbreviation	Name	Hebrew Name
Matt	Matthew	Mattityahu
Mark	Mark	Mark
Luke	Luke	Luke
John	John	Yochanan
Acts	Acts	Acts of the Emissaries
Rom	Romans	Romans
1–2 Cor	1–2 Corinthians	1–2 Corinthians
Gal	Galatians	Galatians
Eph	Ephesians	Ephesians
Phil	Philippians	Philippians
Col	Colossians	Colossians

Abbreviation	Name	Hebrew Name
1–2 Thess	1–2 Thessalonians	1–2 Thessalonians
1–2 Tim	1–2 Timothy	1–2 Timothy
Titus	Titus	Titus
Phlm	Philemon	Philemon
Heb	Hebrews	Messianic Jews
Jas	James	Ya'akov
1–2 Pet	1–2 Peter	1–2 Kefa
1–2–3 John	1–2–3 John	1–2–3 Yochanan
Jude	Jude	Y'hudah
Rev	Revelation	Revelation

SAMPLE HORNER BOOKMARKS

The next pages are samples of the Horner Bookmarks. You can also find a printable version of these bookmarks on the Interfaithfulness website:

https://www.interfaithfulness.org/HornerBookmarks.pdf

Bookmark 1
Genesis, Exodus, Leviticus,
Numbers, Deuteronomy

Bookmark 2
Joshua, Judges, Ruth,
I–II Samuel, I–II Kings

Bookmark 3
I–II Chronicles, Ezra,
Nehemiah, Esther

Bookmark 4
Job, Proverbs, Ecclesiastes,
Song of Songs

Bookmark 5
Psalms
(Read three a day.)

Bookmark 6

Isaiah, Jeremiah, Lamentations, Ezekiel, Daniel

Bookmark 7

Hosea, Joel, Amos, Obadiah, Jonah, Micah, Nahum, Habakkuk, Zephaniah, Haggai, Zechariah, Malachi

Bookmark 8

Matthew, Mark, Luke, John, Acts

Bookmark 9

Romans, I–II Cor, Galatians, Ephesians, Philippians, Colossians, I–II Thessalonians, I–II Timothy, Titus, Philemon, Hebrews, James, I–II Peter, I–II–III John, Jude, Revelation

Bookmark 10

Favorite books, or those you especially want to master.

- _____
- _____

NOTES

Chapter 1

1. One might say that the conversation is always somewhere in between ourselves and God—sometimes more with ourselves, sometimes more with God. Avraham ben Yaakov, *Under the Table & How to Get Up: Jewish Pathways of Spiritual Growth.* https://www.azamra.org/indik/who.htm

2. https://www.jhom.com/topics/firsts/siddur.html

3. "Prayer: Introduction—Why pray in a traditional Jewish manner?" https://ourrabbis.org/main/index.php?option=com_content&view=article&id=22&Itemid=36. (Found online May 29, 2022).

4. Yitzhak Buxbaum speaks of this in his excellent little book, *Real Davvening: Jewish Prayer as a Spiritual Practice and a Form of Meditation for Beginning and Experienced Davveners.* (CreateSpace Independent Publishing Platform, 2015).

5. To find the Torah and *Haftarah* portions for the week, visit www.hebcal.com. At the top of the page you will find the word *"Parashat"* followed by another Hebrew word, both as

hypertext. As you click there, you will come to a page that tells you the Torah reading for the week (also in hypertext), and further down the page, the *Haftarah* reading, also in hypertext. You may choose to use their versions of these readings, or simply look them up in your Bible. For the New Covenant reading, visit https://ourrabbis.org/main/resources/chayyei-yeshua-reading-cycle, and print out a copy of the New Covenant reading cycle provided as a PDF at the bottom of the page. These readings are coordinated with the Hebrew name of each Shabbat, which is the second Hebrew word you noted at the top of the Hebcal page. All of this sounds complex in writing, but after you have done this once or twice, the process is automatic.

6. Rabbi Phillip Sigal wrote that he believed the *Alenu* prayer, formerly only done at *Rosh Hashana*, may have been added to the daily liturgy as a rabbinic reaction to Paul's statements about Yeshua found in Philippians, Chapter 2, which may itself be a *midrash*, an imaginative meditation on the *Alenu* by Paul or other Jewish believers in Yeshua of the time. Phillip Sigal, "Early Christian and Rabbinic Liturgical Affinities: Exploring Liturgical Acculturation," *New Test. Stud.* vol. 30, pp. 75–78.

7. Until the twentieth century, the norm was that only Jewish men aged thirteen or over were to be counted a *minyan*, the accepted quorum indicating the community was meeting for prayer. In 1922, the brilliant iconoclastic rabbi-scholar Mordecai Kaplan changed things by calling his twelve-year-old daughter, Judith, up to read from the Torah on a Shabbat morning. This was the first *Bat Mitzvah* and has become the custom of all but

Orthodox Jewish communities. But even there, changes are afoot in some Orthodox circles favoring egalitarians *minyans*, and what is termed "Open Orthodoxy" or "Progressive Orthodoxy."

Chapter 2

1. George Orwell, "In Front of Your Nose," Tribune, March 22, 1946, in Orwell's *Facing Unpleasant Facts: Narrative Essays* (Boston: Mariner Books, 2009), 213. Compiled by George Packer.

2. Arthur Conan Doyle, *The Hound of the Baskervilles*, Aladdin Classics (New York: Aladdin Paperbacks, 2000), 36.

3. Simons and Chabris, "Selective Attention Test," 1999. Retrieved May 15, 2018 from https://www.youtube.com/results?search_query=simons+chabris

4. For a broader understanding of the phenomenon, see Siri Carpenter, "Sights Unseen," Monitor on Psychology, American Psychological Association, April 2001, Vol. 32, No. 4 found online March 26, 2018, https://www.apa.org/monitor/apr01/blindness.aspx

5. I have written a detailed monograph on this study method, *The Jewish Advantage*, available via Amazon. Contact us at info@interfaithfulness.org to discuss presenting a workshop on havruta study in your context.

6. *Journal of Jewish Education*, 76:3 (215–245). Page numbers referenced in this chapter correspond with an online copy of Kent's article found at https://www.brandeis.edu/mandel/pdfs/TheoryofHavrutaLearning.pdf. Accessed September 26, 2018.

7. Kent, 1

8. Kent, 8

9. Loc. Cit.

10. Kent, 8–9

11. Kent, 9

Chapter 3

1. Mark Kinzer, *Taming the Tongue* (Marshfield, MO: First Fruits of Zion) 2015.

2. Joseph Telushkin, *Words That Hurt, Words That Heal: How to Choose Words Wisely and Well* (New York: W. Morrow and Co., 1996).

3. Telushkin, Joseph. *Words That Hurt, Words That Heal: How the Words You Choose Shape Your Destiny* (New York, NY: William Morrow, an imprint of HarperCollins Publishers, 2019), 28–30.

4. To read of Ladd's stunning achievements and his disastrous fall, see John A. D'Elia, *A Place at the Table: George Eldon Ladd and the Rehabilitation of Evangelical Scholarship in America* (Oxford: Oxford University Press, 2008).

5. For a taste of the breadth of discussion on these matters, visit https://halachipedia.com/index.php?title=Lashon_Hara And there are MANY other sources as well!

6. You can learn more about this by visiting https://www.rivertonshul.org/mussar-what-is-it

Chapter 4

1. Neal Rees, "Snatch Others from the Fire and Save Them: An Examination of Belief in Hell as a Motivating Factor in Missions." Unpublished paper, originally submitted as a term paper to William Carey International University. I mention his paper in this column: http://www.messianicjudaism.me/agenda/2011/09/14/post-missionary-messianic-jewish-outreach-5-did-the-apostles-preach-to-jews-how-to-find-heaven-and-avoid-hell-message/

Rees states further that using the prospect of others going to hell as a goad for missionary action or financial support "succeeds only in producing feelings of self-condemnation rather than considered and solid commitment." Many find such statements so threatening to the status quo that they feel obliged to fight them off and denounce them. But if evidence matters at all, Rees is right.

Chapter 5

1. Gerry Spence, *How To Argue and Win Every Time.* (New York: St. Martin's Griffin, 1996), 119

2. Carmine Gallo, "The Art of the Elevator Pitch," *Harvard Business Review*, found online at https://hbr.org/2018/10/the-art-of-the-elevator-pitch, October 10, 2018.

3. Gregory S. Koukl, *Tactics: A Guide to Effectively Discussing Your Christian Convictions.* (Grand Rapids: Zondervan, 2016).

Chapter 6

1. I deal with this extensively in the first chapter of *Converging Destinies: Jews, Christians, and the Mission of God* (Eugene: Wipf and Stock, 2017).

2. Philip F. Esler, "Ancient Oleiculture and Ethnic Differentiation: The Meaning of the Olive-Tree Image in Romans 11," *Journal for The Study of The New Testament*, 2003, 26. 103–124.

Chapter 8

1. *American Heritage® Dictionary of the English Language.* 5th ed. Houghton Mifflin Harcourt, 2016. All rights reserved.

2. To learn more about this ritual see here: https://www.myjewishlearning.com/recipe/taking-challah/ But in this area

as in so many others, standards of practice are best discerned and pursued in communities that take such matters seriously and follow a common standard of practice. Among Jews who follow the More Jewish Jesus, one of those communities is the Messianic Jewish Rabbinical Council, an association of leaders committed to developing responsible standards in all aspects of Jewish life and to implementing those standards in their congregations. On their webpage, under "Standards" you may find considerable detail on the matters addressed in this book, including the laws of kashrut. Don't be intimidated, but DO be informed. Visit https://ourrabbis.org/main/halakhah-mainmenu-26/kashrut-mainmenu-34

Chapter 9

1. oasis. (n.d.) *American Heritage® Dictionary of the English Language*, 5th ed. (2011). Retrieved from https://www.thefreedictionary.com/oasis

2. William Shakespeare, *Macbeth*, Act 5, Scene 5

3. Thomas Cahill, *The Gifts of the Jews : How a Tribe of Desert Nomads Changed the Way Everyone Thinks and Feels* (New York: Nan A. Talese/Anchor Books, 1999), 144.

4. Cahill, 144.

5. Ronald L. Eisenberg, *The JPS Guide to Jewish Traditions*, JPS Guide (Philadelphia: Jewish Publication Society, 2004), 130.

6. Eisenberg, JPS Guide, 130.

7. Wikipedia says it briefly and well: "The Talmud has two components; the Mishnah (הנשמ, c. 200 CE), a written compendium of the Oral Torah; and the Gemara (ארמג, c. 500 CE), an elucidation of the Mishnah and...writings that often ventures onto other subjects and expounds broadly on the Hebrew Bible. The term "Talmud" may refer to either the Gemara alone, or the Mishnah and Gemara together. (https://en.wikipedia.org/wiki/Talmud)

8. Again, consult the website from the Messianic Jewish Rabbinical Council, the best place I know of to get respectful and reliable input on halachic living integrated around the More Jewish Jesus. See https://ourrabbis.org/main/

9. The halachic standards for Shabbat observance of the Messianic Jewish Rabbinical Council (MJRC) comment helpfully about a certain relational, family-honoring flexibility: "In general, traveling on Shabbat conflicts with the spirit of the day. Nevertheless, limited travel may be appropriate to uphold certain values that are themselves associated with Shabbat. Thus, our basic practice does not prohibit travel on Shabbat to attend services at the synagogue, to visit the sick, and to sustain contact with the synagogue community and with one's family, though such travel should not occupy a substantial portion of the day. Normally one should avoid traveling on Shabbat for other purposes." Shabbat 4.1.8 (Traveling) found online, March 18, 2018, at https://ourrabbis.org/main/index.php?option=com_content&view=article&id=16&Itemid=30

10. Sherry Turkle, *Alone Together: Why We Expect More from Technology and Less from Each Other* (New York: Basic Books, 2012), 1.

11. MJRC Standards, section 4.1.9 Food Preparation found on line 3/27/18 at https://ourrabbis.org/main/documents/MJRC_Standards_Aug2011.pdf

12. Lyrics by Sheldon Harnick from the 1964 Broadway play *Fiddler on the Roof*, later made famous in 1971 by the movie of the same name.

Chapter 10

1. Bernard Reisman, *The Chavurah: A Contemporary Jewish Experience*, (n.p., URJ Press, 1977).

2. Priya Parker, *The Art of Gathering: How We Meet and Why It Matters*, New York: Riverhead Books, 2018), 43.

3. Alan Hirsch develops this mindset of focusing on functions rather than offices in his book *5Q : Reactivating the Original Intelligence and Capacity of the Body of Christ* (100 Movements, 2017). I am indebted to this book for how I now approach these matters, making some adaptations of my own.

Chapter 11

1. For a *complete* list of major and minor holidays, see https://www.hebcal.com/holidays/ where you will also find

links to articles about each of these occasions. You might also consult Wikipedia at https://en.wikipedia.org/wiki/Jewish_holidays and https://www.jewfaq.org/holiday0.htm which also includes hypertext links to excellent articles about each of the holidays.

2. In Israel, families and friends gather together for a bonfire or a picnic on Lag Ba'Omer, often on Mount Meron. Some people in the Diaspora hold events as well. One opinion is that this is done to honor the memory of Rabbi Shimon Bar Yochai, whose mystical work, the Zohar, was thought of as bringing great light to the world. Another explanation focuses on the Bar Kochba revolt against Roman rule, 132–136 CE. The Romans had forbidden the setting of bonfires which were used to signal the beginning of a new month, important for religious purposes. The Romans sought to undermine Jewish religious life. When Bar Kochba's ultimately failed revolt was first successful, the use of such bonfires was reinstituted. So, we do this now in commemoration.

On Lag Ba'Omer kids go out into the fields to play with bows and arrows. There are two schools of thought as to what this custom commemorates. One opinion cited in the Midrash is that during the time of Rabbi Shimon Bar Yochai, no rainbow was seen. God promised Noah that he would never again bring a devastating flood upon the world. The rainbow, according to Talmudic commentators, appears when God deems the people of the world as deserving severe punishment for wrongdoing. It was due to Rabbi Shimon Bar Yochai's merit that the world was protected from punishment and the warning significance of the rainbow was discontinued. The other reason given for youngsters going out into the fields to shoot arrows is that it commemorates Bar Kochba's temporary victory over the Romans.

It is customary in some Jewish communities to eat carobs on Lag Ba'Omer to commemorate the miracle that occurred to Rabbi Shimon Bar Yochai and his son while they were hiding in the cave, after fleeing Roman persecution. For thirteen years, Rabbi Shimon and his son sustained themselves on carobs and water from a tree and spring that God had miraculously provided for them.

Even if we do not believe in such legendary stories, we should know and respect how they embody truths important to our people. We don't always have to agree. But we should always show respect.

Chapter 12

1. Retrieved from http://hashivenu.org/core-value-7/

2. *Collins English Dictionary—Complete and Unabridged, 12th Ed., 2014.* S.v. "hapax legomenon." Retrieved April 2, 2018 from https://www.thefreedictionary.com/hapax+legomenon

3. A way to visually organize information as developed by Tony Buzan.

FOR FURTHER READING

Artson, Bradley Shavit. 1995. *It's a Mitzvah! Step-by-Step to Jewish Living*. West Orange, NJ: Behrman House.

Banks, Robert J. 2012. *Paul's Idea of Community: The Early House Churches in Their Cultural Setting*. Grand Rapids, MI: Baker Academic.

Banks, Robert J., and Julia Banks. 1998. *The Church Comes Home*. Peabody, MA: Hendrickson.

Bates, Matthew W. 2017. *Salvation by Allegiance Alone: Rethinking Faith, Works, and the Gospel of Jesus the King*. Grand Rapids, MI: Baker Academic.

Bauer, David R., and Robert A. Traina. 2014. *Inductive Bible Study: A Comprehensive Guide to the Practice of Hermeneutics*. Grand Rapids, MI: Baker Academic.

Bloch, Abraham P. 1978. *The Biblical and Historical Background of the Jewish Holy Days*. Brooklyn, NY: KTAV Publishing House.

Bloch, Abraham P. 1980. *The Biblical and Historical Background of Jewish Customs and Ceremonies.* Brooklyn, NY: KTAV Publishing House.

Bock, Darrell L., and Mitch Glaser, eds. 2013. *The Gospel According to Isaiah 53: Encountering the Suffering Servant in Jewish and Christian Theology.* Grand Rapids, MI: Kregel Publications.

Brown, Michael L. 2000–2010. *Answering Jewish Objections to Jesus.* Grand Rapids, MI: Baker Books. (Five volumes).

Budoff, Barry. 1999. *A Messianic Jewish Siddur for Shabbat, in Hebrew and English.* 4th ed. Clarksville, MD: Messianic Jewish Publishers & Resources.

Dauermann, Stuart. November 21, 2018. "Six Encounters: Axes of Spiritual Transformation." https://www.interfaithfulness.org/six-encounters-axes-of-spiritual-transformation/.

Dauermann, Stuart. 2009. *Christians and Jews Together.* Eugene, OR: Wipf and Stock.

Dauermann, Stuart. 2018. *The Jewish Advantage: What It Is—and How to Make It Your Own.* Altadena, CA: Interfaithfulness.

Deere, Jack. 2020. *Why I Am Still Surprised by the Power of the Spirit: Discovering How God Speaks and*

Heals Today, rev. ed. Grand Rapids, MI: Zondervan Reflective.

Donin, Hayim. H. 2019. *To Pray as a Jew: A Guide to the Prayer Book and the Synagogue Service.* New York: Basic Books.

Fee, Gordon D. 1996. *Paul, the Spirit, and the People of God.* Grand Rapids, MI: Baker Academic.

Fee, Gordon D. 2012. *God's Empowering Presence: The Holy Spirit in the Letters of Paul.* Reprint edition, Grand Rapids, MI: Baker Academic.

Feldman, Daniel Z. 2015. *False Facts and True Rumors: Lashon HaRa in Contemporary Culture.* New Milford, CT: Maggid Books.

Fisher, John, and David Bronstein. 1988. *Sidur li-Yehudim Meshihim (Siddur for Messianic Jews).* Palm Harbor, FL: Menorah Ministries.

Foster, Richard J. 2002. *Prayer: Finding the Heart's True Home.* New York: HarperOne.

Frishman, Elyse D., ed. 2007. *Mishkan T'filah: A Reform Siddur, non-transliterated (Shabbat, Weekdays + Festivals).* New York: CCAR Press. https://ccarpress.org/shopping_product_detail.asp?pid=50203.

Garfiel, Evelyn. 1977. *Service of the Heart: A Guide to the Jewish Prayer Book*. Reprint, Lanham, MD: Jason Aronson.

Glaser, Mitch, and Zhava Glaser. 1987. *The Fall Feasts of Israel*. Chicago: Moody Press.

Green, Arthur. 1992. *Tormented Master: The Life and Spiritual Quest of Rabbi Nahman of Bratslav*. Woodstock, VT: Jewish Lights.

Greenbaum, Avraham. 1991. *Under the Table & How to Get Up: Jewish Pathways of Spiritual Growth*. Monsey, NY: Breslov Research Institute.

Greenberg, Irving. 1988. *The Jewish Way: Living the Holidays*. New York: Summit Books.

Haase, Albert. 2019. *Becoming an Ordinary Mystic: Spirituality for the Rest of Us*. Downers Grove, IL: InterVarsity Press.

Hendricks, Howard G., and William D. Hendricks. (2014). *Living by the Book: The Art and Science of Reading the Bible*. Chicago: Moody. (Set of 2 books—book and workbook, paperback.)

Heschel, Abraham J. 1951. *The Sabbath, Its Meaning for Modern Man*. New York: Farrar, Straus and Young.

Hirsch, Alan. 2017. *5Q : Reactivating the Original Intelligence and Capacity of the Body of Christ*. N.p.: 100 Movements.

Hoffman, Lawrence A. 1999. *The Art of Public Prayer: Not for Clergy Only*. Woodstock, VT: SkyLight Paths.

Holzer, Elie. 2014. *A Philosophy of Havruta: Understanding and Teaching the Art of Text Study in Pairs*. With Orit Kent. Brookline, MA: Academic Studies Press.

Kagen, Yisroel Meir. 2015. *Sefer Chofetz Chaim—English Translation Arranged for Daily Study*. Lakewood, NJ: Israel Bookshop.

Kasdan, Barney. 2007. *God's Appointed Times: A Practical Guide to Understanding and Celebrating the Biblical Holy Days*. Clarksville, MD: Lederer Books.

Keener, Craig S. 1996. *3 Crucial Questions about the Holy Spirit*. Grand Rapids, MI: Baker Publishing Group.

Keener, Craig S. 2020. *Gift and Giver: The Holy Spirit for Today*. Grand Rapids, MI: Baker Academic.

Kinzer, Mark S. 2005. *Postmissionary Messianic Judaism: Redefining Christian Engagement with the Jewish People*. Grand Rapids, MI: Brazos Press.

Kinzer, Mark S. 2018. *Jerusalem Crucified, Jerusalem Risen: The Resurrected Messiah, the Jewish People, and the Land of Promise.* Eugene, OR: Cascade Books.

Kinzer, Mark S. 2015. *Taming the Tongue.* Marshfield, MO: First Fruits of Zion.

Kinzer, Mark S., and Russell L. Resnik. 2021. *Besorah: The Resurrection of Jerusalem and the Healing of a Fractured Gospel.* Eugene, OR: Cascade Books.

Kinzer, Mark S. 2012. *Israel's Messiah and the People of God: a Vision for Messianic Jewish Covenant Fidelity.* Edited by Jennifer M. Rosner. Cambridge, UK: Lutterworth Press.

Kinzer, Mark S. 2015. *Searching Her Own Mystery: Nostra Aetate, the Jewish People, and the Identity of the Church.* Eugene, OR: Cascade Books.

Koukl, Gregory. 2019. *Tactics, 10th Anniversary Edition: A Game Plan for Discussing Your Christian Convictions.* Grand Rapids, MI: Zondervan Reflective.

Kraft, Charles H., "What Kind of Encounters Do We Need in Our Christian Witness?" Missio Nexus (online membership Christian community), July 1, 1991, https://missionexus.org/what-kind-of-encounters-do-we-need-in-our-christian-witness/.

Stuart Dauermann

Lloyd-Jones, David Martyn. 1985. *Joy Unspeakable: Power & Renewal in the Holy Spirit*. Edited by Christopher Catherwood. Wheaton, IL: Harold Shaw.

McKnight, Scot. 2011. *The King Jesus Gospel: The Original Good News Revisited*. Grand Rapids, MI: Zondervan.

Messianic Jewish Rabbinical Council (discussion on *kashrut*): https://ourrabbis.org/main/halakhah-mainmenu-26/kashrut-mainmenu-34.

Messianic Jewish Rabbinical Council (statement of Jewish standards of observance): https://ourrabbis.org/main/documents/MJRC_Standards_Aug2014.pdf.

Messianic Jewish Rabbinical Council, "Prayer: Introduction—Why pray in a traditional Jewish manner?" https://ourrabbis.org/main/halakhah-main-menu-26/halakhic-introduction/halakhic-introduction-2. (scroll down to Table of Contents)

Miller, Paul E. 2017. *A Praying Life: Connecting with God in a Distracting World*. Carol Stream, IL: NavPress.

Miller, Paul E. 2019. *Beginning a Praying Life*. Carol Stream, IL: NavPress.

Nadler, Sam. 2007. *Messiah in the Feasts of Israel.* Charlotte, NC: Rose Publishing.

National Havurah Committee website: https://havurah.org/.

Noordmans, Philip. J. 2016. *FireStarter: The Holy Spirit Empowers.* N.p.: Stewardship Enterprises.

Parker, Priya. 2018. *The Art of Gathering: How We Meet and Why It Matters.* New York: Riverhead Books.

Prell, Riv-Ellen. 1989. *Prayer & Community: The Havurah in American Judaism.* Detroit, MI: Wayne State University Press.

Pressman, Daniel, and Ronald Isaacs. 2011. *Siddur Or Shalom Le-Shabbat Ve-Yom Tov (Siddur Or Shalom for Shabbat and Festivals).* Jersey City, NJ: KTAV Publishing House.

Pullinger, Jackie 2007. *Chasing the Dragon: One Woman's Struggle Against the Darkness of Hong Kong's Drug Dens.* With Andrew Quicke. Bloomington, MN: Chosen Books.

Reisman, Bernard. 1977. *The Chavurah: A Contemporary Jewish Experience.* N.p.: URJ Press.

Rosenberg, Arnold S. 2000. *Jewish Liturgy as a Spiritual System: A Prayer-by-Prayer Explanation of the Na-*

ture and Meaning of Jewish Worship. Lanham, MD: Jason Aronson.

Roussel, Isaac. S. 2017. *Shabbat Siddur: Siddur Kehillat Zera Avraham*. N.p.: CreateSpace.

Rydelnik, Michael, and Edward Blum, eds. 2019. *The Moody Handbook of Messianic Prophecy: Studies and Expositions of the Messiah in the Old Testament*. Chicago: Moody.

Shapiro, Mark Dov, ed. 2016. *Gates of Shabbat [Sha'arei Shabbat]: A Guide for Observing Shabbat*. Revised edition, New York: Central Conference of American Rabbis (CCAR Press).

Simmons, Annette. 2007. *Whoever Tells the Best Story Wins: How to Use Your Own Stories to Communicate with Power and Impact*. New York: Amacom.

Strassfeld, Michael, Betsy Platkin Teutsch, & Arnold M. Eisen. 1985. *The Jewish Holidays: A Guide and Commentary*. New York: Harper & Row.

Telushkin, Joseph. 2019. *Words That Hurt, Words That Heal: How the Words You Choose Shape Your Destiny*, rev. ed. New York: William Morrow.

Thurston, Bonnie. 2009. *For God Alone: A Primer on Prayer*. University of Notre Dame Press.

Traina, Robert A. 2002. *Methodical Bible Study*. Grand Rapids, MI: Zondervan Academic.

Wagner, Jordan Lee. 2013. *The Synagogue Survival Kit: A Guide to Understanding Jewish Religious Services*. Lanham, MD: Jason Aronson.

Wolfson, Ron. 1985. *Seder lel Shabat [The Shabbat Seder]*. New York: Federation of Jewish Men's Clubs and the University of Judaism.

Wolfson, Ron. 2002. *Shabbat: The Family Guide to Preparing for and Celebrating the Sabbath*, 2nd ed. Woodstock, VT: Jewish Lights.

Wolfson, Ron. 2013. *Relational Judaism: Using the Power of Relationships to Transform the Jewish Community*. Woodstock, VT: Jewish Lights.

ALSO BY DR. STUART DAUERMANN

Converging Destinies: Jews, Christians, and the Mission of God examines how the Jewish world and the Christian world have been accustomed to view each other and their responsibilities toward each other under the *missio dei*, the mission of God, that is, what God is up to in the world. The book calls for a recognition of God's foundational calling upon the Jews as home base of the people of God, and calls both the Jewish world and the church to adjust how they speak to and of each other, and listen to each other in view of their mutual accountability to God as agents of his purpose. In view of this accountability, we are called to stand in awe of God and his purpose, humbly vulnerable to what he would say to us, even through the lips of the other.

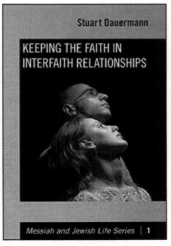

Keeping the Faith in Interfaith Relationships shows but one way among others that a Christian spouse and a Jewish one can both honor their convictions, while having a unified home. Not everyone will choose the path taken here, but all will find this artfully presented series of conversations real food for thought. Many interdating couples and intermarried people will find much to discuss in these pages.

Son of David: Healing the Vision of the Messianic Jewish Movement presents a biblical view of God's consummating purposes for the Jewish people. This monograph challenges the Messianic Jewish movement to "get with the program" rather than serving more trendy and derivative agendas. One of the core questions answered here is this: What would the gospel look like if it was good news for the Jews?

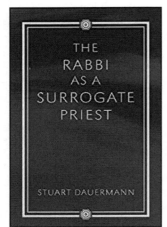

The Rabbi as a Surrogate Priest, Dr Dauermann's dissertation, compares the role of the rabbi as it has emerged in Jewish life to the roles performed by priests and Levites as found in biblical materials. Beginning with Abraham, viewed as a proto-priest, the dissertation examines the functions performed by Israel's priests and Levites within the context of Israel's call to be a kingdom of priests and a holy nation. The work traces the historical evolution of the rabbi's role and of the training of rabbis, and identifies sixteen functions formerly performed by priests and Levites which now describe what rabbis do. The book will come as a surprise to people who imagine the rabbi's role to be "unbliblical," and also as a help to those who seek to train leaders to see that a rabbi is not just a minister with switched labels.

The Jewish Advantage: What It Is and How to Make It Your Own provides a proven solution to the general subpar state of biblical illiteracy—even among the religiously committed.

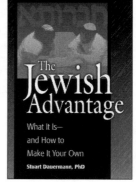

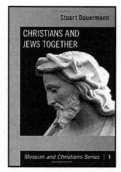

Christians and Jews Together presents a biblical argument for the complementary roles Jews and Christians are meant to play in the outworking of God's purposes moving toward His great consummation. It is as if God has given Jews and Christians half of a treasure map: neither of them can find the treasure of God's consummation apart from the other. For Christians, this book asks and answers the question: What's greater than the great commission? Prepare to be informed, challenged, and intrigued.

Made in the USA
Middletown, DE
05 September 2023

38065581R00208